AI FOR ABSOLUTE BEGINNERS

EASY GUIDE WITH CLEAR EXPLANATIONS AND REAL-WORLD APPLICATIONS OF ARTIFICIAL INTELLIGENCE TO QUICKLY GAIN CONFIDENCE—NO TECH SKILLS REQUIRED

AVA SINCLAIR

CONTENTS

INTRODUCTION

In the bustling streets of a modern city, a young professional named Lila navigates her daily life with the help of seemingly mundane tools. Her smartphone suggests the quickest route to work, her favorite streaming service recommends a new series based on her viewing history, and her email inbox automatically filters out spam. Lila may not realize that these conveniences are powered by artificial intelligence (AI), quietly working behind the scenes to simplify and enhance her experiences.

As an author, I was in a similar position to Lila not long ago. AI seemed daunting, reserved for tech experts and science fiction novels. However, as I began to explore the subject, I discovered that AI is not only accessible but also increasingly relevant to our everyday lives. This realization ignited my passion to demystify AI for others who, like Lila and myself, may feel intimidated by its complexity.

"AI for Absolute Beginners" aims to bridge the gap between curiosity and confidence. With this book, I want to eliminate the barriers that often prevent people from engaging with AI, such as technical jargon, complex concepts, and the misconception that AI is irrelevant to their lives. I aim to create a welcoming and informative introduction to this transformative technology by breaking down AI into simple, relatable ideas and providing practical examples.

This book is specifically tailored for adults curious about AI but lacking a technical background. It addresses the common concerns beginners face, such as the fear of not understanding technical terms, uncertainty about how AI applies to daily life, and apprehension about job security in an AI-driven future. By directly addressing these concerns and providing clear explanations, this book wants to empower you, my readers, to engage with AI confidently. Each chapter focuses on a key aspect of AI, from its basic concepts and history to its practical applications and future implications. I structured the content to provide a logical progression of knowledge, with clear explanations, real-world examples, and hands-on activities that reinforce learning.

As you delve into the pages of this book, you will discover the importance of understanding AI in today's rapidly evolving world. AI is no longer a distant concept; it is a reality that influences nearly every aspect of our lives. From healthcare and education to finance and entertainment, AI is transforming the way we live, work, and interact with one another. By gaining a foundational understanding of AI, you will be better equipped to navigate this changing landscape and harness the potential of this powerful technology.

I invite you to actively engage with the content, take part in the exercises, reflect on the examples, and consider how AI can be applied to your life and career. This book is not just a passive reading experience; it is an opportunity to take ownership of your learning journey and develop a practical understanding of AI.

Finally, you may also be wondering about the extent to which AI contributed to this book. I can honestly say that AI—specifically, ChatGPT—played a role in its development. Throughout the writing process, I collaborated with ChatGPT to refine this manuscript, seeing it as an instant editor, a creative writing companion, and a valuable advisor. ChatGPT helped me brainstorm ideas, structure the flow of chapters, and enhance the overall narrative to ensure the best possible reading experience for you. By the time you finish this book, I believe you will appreciate these benefits and gain numerous ideas on how to integrate AI tools into your daily and professional life to simplify and enhance your workflow.

So, let us begin this exploration of artificial intelligence together as we uncover the fascinating world of AI and its limitless possibilities.

1

UNDERSTANDING THE BASICS OF AI

As you sit in your living room, perhaps scrolling through your smartphone, you might notice how the device intuitively knows what content you are interested in. It might suggest a new video to watch or a novel to read, seemingly reading your preferences without explicit guidance. This phenomenon is not magic; it's artificial intelligence at work, seamlessly woven into your everyday experience. AI has become integral to modern life, even if its presence often goes unnoticed. This chapter aims to illuminate the foundational concepts of AI, dispel the aura of complexity around it, and equip you with the knowledge to recognize and appreciate the AI-driven transformations happening around you. I invite you to actively engage with the material, challenge your understanding, and consider how you can integrate AI into your life and work. By taking this first step, you are opening the door to a wealth of possibilities AI offers.

1.1 WHAT IS AI? SIMPLIFYING LANGUAGE AND TACKLING TECHNICAL JARGON

To begin understanding AI, we must first address the terminology that often makes it appear inaccessible. Key terms like "algorithm," "neural network," "machine learning," and "natural language processing" frequently surface in discussions about AI. These words seem daunting, but you can break their meanings into simpler concepts.

Understanding these terms is crucial because they form the backbone of AI technology. By breaking down the jargon into relatable analogies, I aim to make AI accessible to everyone, regardless of technical background. As I progress through this book, you will encounter these terms repeatedly, and hopefully, they will feel less intimidating as you see them applied in various contexts. AI is not just a tool for scientists and engineers; it is a transformative technology reshaping industries and daily life.

An algorithm is a set of instructions designed to perform a specific task or solve a problem. You can think of it like a recipe a chef might follow to create a dish. Just as a recipe provides step-by-step guidance on combining ingredients to produce a meal, an algorithm offers a series of steps for a computer to follow to achieve a desired outcome. This analogy clarifies that algorithms are not inherently complex or mysterious; they are structured methods for solving problems.

Let's examine the three other key AI concepts: neural networks, machine learning, and natural language processing. These technologies play a crucial role in how AI systems function, and the following sections will explore how they work and why they are so powerful.

Neural Networks: The Brain Behind AI

Neural networks are another cornerstone of AI. They might sound like a complex scientific term, but at their core, they are inspired by the human brain's architecture. Imagine the brain's neurons—billions of interconnected cells that process information and allow us to think and learn. Neural networks in AI mimic this biological structure by creating layers of interconnected nodes or artificial neurons —tiny nerve cells— that collaborate to process data. These networks learn from the data they encounter, adjusting their internal parameters like our brain strengthens synaptic connections through experiences.

Just as neurons form networks through synapses, neural networks in AI consist of nodes and layers that work together to process data and make decisions. Like neurons, these nodes are organized into layers, each fulfilling a specific role in the information processing chain. The input layer receives raw data, the hidden layers perform complex transformations and computations, and the output layer produces the final result or prediction. Understanding this structure helps demystify how these networks function and reveal their potential to perform tasks that were once thought exclusive to human cognition.

What helped me most is to imagine that neural networks operate like a series of interconnected highways, each representing a pathway through which information travels. Data enters the network via the input layer, akin to cars entering a freeway. This data is then processed through hidden layers, where each node functions like a checkpoint, analyzing and transforming the information based on its internal parameters, known as weights and biases. These parameters, like traffic signals, adjust dynamically, directing the data flow to achieve accurate and efficient outcomes. The hidden layers are where the magic happens, enabling the network to learn and refine its skills through training. Finally, the processed data exits through the output layer, yielding predictions or decisions that the network has derived from its internal computations. This process is iterative; neural networks learn by adjusting their weights and biases over many iterations, honing their accuracy and effectiveness with each cycle.

In practical terms, neural networks power various applications that have become integral to modern life. One prominent example is facial recognition technology, which uses neural networks to identify and verify individuals based on their facial features. By analyzing an image's geometric structure and pixel patterns, these networks can match a face to a stored image database, enabling everything from securing smartphones to enhancing airport security. Voice assistants like Google Assistant also rely heavily on neural networks. They interpret and process spoken language, converting it into actionable commands. These assistants utilize neural networks to understand context and semantics, allowing them to respond accurately to user queries. Additionally, neural networks contribute to predictive analytics in marketing, helping businesses anticipate consumer behavior and tailor their marketing strategies accordingly. These networks can predict future trends and preferences by analyzing vast customer data, enabling more personalized and effective marketing campaigns.

Despite their versatility, neural networks face several challenges that can impede their development and deployment. One significant barrier is the need for large datasets to train these models effectively. Just as a person requires extensive experience to develop expertise, neural networks need vast data to learn patterns and make reliable predictions. Without sufficient data, these networks may struggle to generalize their learning to new situations, limiting their applicability. Additionally, the computational demands of training and running neural networks are considerable. These models require substantial processing power and memory, often necessitating specialized hardware and infrastructure. As a result, developing and deploying neural networks can be resource-intensive and costly, posing a challenge for smaller organizations and those with limited technical resources.

In conclusion, neural networks represent a remarkable fusion of biological inspiration and computational innovation, enabling machines to perform tasks that were once the sole domain of human intelligence. By mimicking the brain's structure and function, these networks have unlocked new possibilities in security to marketing, transforming how we interact with technology and data. However, the journey from concept to application is fraught with challenges, emphasizing the need for robust datasets and powerful computational tools. As we continue to explore the potential of neural networks, we must navigate these obstacles to realize their full promise and potential in shaping the future of artificial intelligence.

Machine Learning: Learning from Data

Machine learning, often abbreviated as ML, is another fundamental concept that underpins much of AI's functionality. Machine learning involves systems that improve over time as they are exposed to more data, similar to how humans learn from experience. Consider how a child learns to recognize animals. Initially, they might only distinguish between a dog and a cat, but their ability to identify different species becomes more refined as they encounter more animals. Machine learning operates on this principle, using algorithms to sift through data, recognize patterns, and make predictions or decisions based on the information it processes. This continuous learning capability makes AI systems more accurate and efficient over time.

Unlike traditional programming, where explicit instructions guide every action, machine learning empowers computers to recognize patterns and make decisions based on data inputs. Imagine it as teaching a computer to identify cats in photos. Instead of telling the computer what a cat looks like, you feed it thousands of images labeled as "cat" or "not cat." Over time, the computer analyzes the patterns that define a cat, such as shape, size, and color, and learns to identify cats in new, unlabeled photos. This ability to learn and adapt is the essence of machine learning.

Machine learning comes in different flavors, each suited to particular problems. Supervised learning is the most intuitive, as it involves training a model on a labeled dataset. The algorithm learns the relationship between input data and the desired output in this approach. Consider a spam filter that distinguishes between legitimate emails and spam. By analyzing a dataset containing examples of both categories, the algorithm learns to predict whether new emails are spam based on their features, such as the presence of certain words or phrases. This method is robust for tasks where historical data provides clear guidance.

In contrast, unsupervised learning deals with data that lacks explicit labels, making the task more exploratory. Here, the goal is to discover hidden patterns or groupings within the data. Picture a vast dataset of customer transactions. Using unsupervised learning, you can identify clusters of similar purchasing behaviors, revealing insights into customer segments without prior knowledge of those categories. This approach is invaluable for market segmentation, anomaly detection, and exploratory data analysis, where the underlying structure of the data is not immediately apparent.

Reinforcement learning introduces a dynamic element, enabling machines to learn through trial and error. It involves an agent interacting with an environment, acting, and receiving feedback through rewards or penalties. Over time, the agent learns to maximize cumulative rewards by refining its strategy. A prime example is training a robot to navigate a maze. Initially, the robot explores different paths randomly. As it receives rewards for reaching the exit, it gradually learns the most efficient route. Reinforcement learning is used in robotics, gaming, and any domain where decision-making in complex, changing environments is critical.

Machine learning's impact is profound and widespread, touching various sectors and applications. In banking, for instance, fraud detection systems leverage machine learning to analyze transaction patterns and flag anomalies indicative of fraudulent activity. These systems continuously update their models as new data comes in, enhancing their ability to detect even subtle, evolving threats. In image recognition, machine learning powers technologies that identify faces in photographs, enabling security systems to verify identities or unlock devices. Such applications underscore machine learning's capacity to process and interpret vast amounts of data, generating insights and automating complex tasks.

The success of machine learning hinges on the quality and quantity of data it receives. The adage "garbage in, garbage out" aptly captures the importance of clean, relevant data. Poor-quality data can lead to inaccurate models and unreliable predictions. Conversely, diverse and comprehensive datasets enable robust learning, allowing models to generalize effectively to new, unseen data. This principle is evident in recommendation systems such as Netflix and Amazon. These systems suggest content or products aligned with individual preferences by analyzing extensive user behavior data, enhancing user satisfaction and engagement.

Machine learning embodies a paradigm shift in computing, where data becomes the raw material for building intelligent systems. Its ability to derive patterns, learn from experience, and adapt to new information empowers technology to solve problems and make decisions in ways previously unimaginable.

Exercise for You: Exploring Your Data

Take a moment to reflect on the data you encounter daily. It might be emails, social media interactions, or even your browsing history. Consider how these data points could be used in a machine learning context. What patterns or insights might an algorithm detect? This exercise encourages you to think about the data-driven nature of our world and how machine learning leverages this wealth of information.

Natural Language Processing: Talking to Machines

When you speak to your digital assistant to play your favorite song or set a meeting reminder, you engage with sophisticated Natural Language Processing (NLP) technology. NLP bridges the gap between human language and machine comprehension, allowing computers to interpret, understand, and respond naturally to spoken or written words. NLP breaks down communication barriers by enabling meaningful interactions between humans and machines, transforming complex commands into intuitive conversations. At its core, NLP revolutionizes our engagement with technology, making interactions seamless and intuitive.

The process of NLP is intricate, comprising several components that work together to facilitate this understanding. One of the fundamental elements is tokenization, which involves dividing text into smaller, manageable units called tokens. Consider it dissecting a sentence into individual words or phrases, allowing the machine to analyze each component separately. This breakdown is crucial for identifying language structure and making sense of its content. Another key aspect of NLP is sentiment analysis, a technique used to determine the emotional tone of a text. By evaluating words and phrases, machines can gauge whether a message conveys positivity, negativity, or neutrality, providing insights into user opinions and feelings. Finally, language generation is the component responsible for creating human-like text based on input data. This capability enables machines to produce coherent and contextually appropriate responses, enhancing the fluidity and naturalness of machine-human interactions.

In our daily lives, NLP powers myriad applications that streamline communication and enhance user experience. Customer service chatbots exemplify the practical use of NLP, as they engage with users to resolve inquiries and provide support. These chatbots leverage language processing to understand user queries, delivering timely and relevant responses. Translation tools, such as Google Translate, also rely heavily on NLP to convert text from one language to another, facilitating cross-cultural communication and bridging linguistic divides. These tools ensure accurate translations that retain the original meaning and context by analyzing the semantics and syntax of languages.

Despite its many successes, NLP faces several challenges that complicate its development and implementation. One of the primary hurdles is understanding context and ambiguity in language. Human communication is rich with nuances, where a single word or phrase can carry multiple meanings depending on the context. Machines must decipher these subtleties to deliver accurate responses, requiring sophisticated algorithms and extensive training data. Additionally, NLP must contend with idiomatic expressions and slang, which can vary widely between cultures and regions. These informal language forms often defy conventional grammar rules, posing a significant challenge for machines attempting to process and understand them accurately.

Despite these obstacles, advancements in NLP continue to make strides, driven by innovations in machine learning and neural networks. Researchers and developers work tirelessly to enhance the capabilities of NLP, enabling machines to understand better and replicate human communication. As these technologies evolve, we can anticipate even more seamless and intuitive interactions with machines, reshaping the landscape of digital communication and connectivity.

Exercise for You: Exploring Everyday NLP

Consider the various digital tools and applications you use daily, such as virtual assistants, chatbots, or language translation apps. Reflect on how NLP enhances your interactions with these technologies. How does the ability to communicate naturally with machines improve your overall experience? This reflection encourages you to appreciate the impact of NLP in your everyday life and recognize its role in transforming human-machine communication.

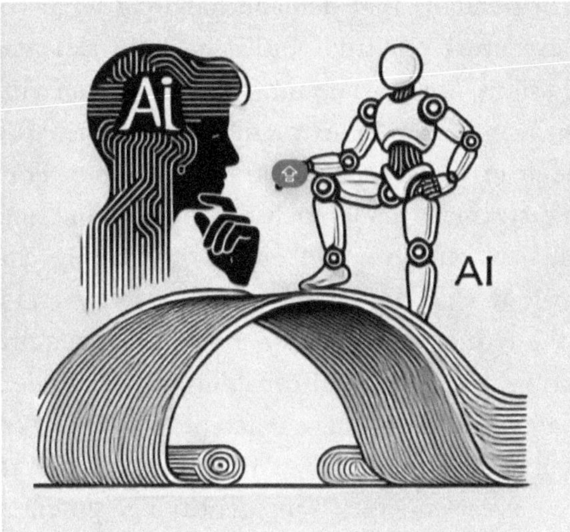

1.2 AI VS. HUMAN INTELLIGENCE: KEY DIFFERENCES

In contemplating the essence of intelligence, one must distinguish between the capabilities of artificial intelligence and those inherent to human cognition. While AI and human intellect aim to solve problems and adapt to new challenges, they do so through disparate mechanisms and with varying strengths. AI is renowned for its speed and precision, executing tasks at a pace and accuracy that far surpass human limits. Consider the computational prowess required to analyze vast datasets in seconds, a feat unattainable by human effort. This ability allows AI to perform complex calculations, identify patterns, and generate insights with unparalleled efficiency. Conversely, human intelligence shines in its capacity for intuition, creativity, and emotional depth. Humans can draw from past experiences, consider abstract concepts, and empathize with others, enriching their problem-solving approaches with a nuanced understanding beyond mere data processing.

AI excels in domains that demand handling large volumes of data and executing repetitive tasks. In industries where data-driven decisions are paramount, AI systems can sift through mountains of information, extracting relevant insights without the fatigue or error associated with human labor. For instance, AI has transformed fields such as finance and logistics by automating data analysis and optimizing supply chains. The precision of AI algorithms ensures consistency and accuracy, reducing the risk of human error in tasks that require meticulous attention to detail. Such capabilities have made AI indispensable in applications where reliability and speed are crucial, like medical diagnostics, where AI can rapidly analyze medical images to assist doctors in identifying potential health concerns.

Despite these strengths, AI confronts limitations that highlight the irreplaceable qualities of human intelligence. A significant constraint lies in AI's lack of emotional understanding and empathy. Machines can process language and generate responses, yet they lack genuine comprehension of human emotions. This deficiency becomes apparent in customer service interactions where a nuanced understanding of tone and context is essential. Humans can interpret and respond to emotional cues, fostering connections that machines cannot replicate.

Additionally, AI struggles with adapting to novel situations without prior data. Human adaptability allows innovation and creativity in uncharted territories, while AI relies heavily on pre-existing data and patterns. This reliance can hinder AI's effectiveness in dynamic environments where conditions change unpredictably.

The future of AI and human intelligence lies in each complementing the other's strengths. AI can be an augmentation tool for human decision-making, providing data-driven insights that enhance human judgment. By automating routine tasks, AI frees humans to focus on creative and strategic endeavors, fostering a collaborative environment where both entities thrive. Collaborative intelligence envisions scenarios where humans and machines work together, leveraging AI's computational power and human ingenuity to tackle complex challenges. This partnership holds promise across various fields, from healthcare and education to art and science, where combining human creativity and AI's analytical capabilities can lead to groundbreaking discoveries and innovations.

As AI continues to evolve, its integration into daily life will become more seamless, reshaping industries and redefining the human experience. However, the distinction between AI and human intelligence remains critical, underscoring the unique contributions each brings to the table. By recognizing these differences, we can harness the potential of AI while preserving the essential qualities that define humanity. This understanding paves the way for a future where technology enhances, rather than replaces, human capabilities, fostering a world where AI and human intelligence coexist harmoniously, each strengthening the other in pursuit of shared goals and aspirations.

Chapter 1 Self-Assessment

Reflecting on what you have learned so far can reinforce knowledge and guide you to areas that may require further exploration. As you have traversed the landscape of artificial intelligence, consider the multifaceted nature of this technology and its profound implications for our world.

Neural networks have offered a glimpse into the architectural marvels inspired by our cognitive processes. These networks are the unsung heroes of many AI applications, silently performing complex computations that mimic the human brain's ability to analyze, learn, and adapt. They have transformed industries by powering tools that recognize faces in photos, understand spoken words, and predict future consumer behavior. Such applications highlight the versatility and power of neural networks, yet they also underscore the challenges posed by their demands for extensive datasets and computational resources. As you ponder these challenges, consider how they shape the development and implementation of AI technologies.

You have encountered machine learning, an intricate system that allows computers to evolve through data exposure, enhancing their predictive capabilities and making more informed decisions over time. Think about how machine learning relies on data quality and diversity—what goes in dictates what comes out, directly shaping its outputs.

Natural Language Processing (NLP) further expands your understanding of AI's capabilities. By bridging the gap between human communication and machine interpretation, NLP enables seamless interactions with technology. It allows machines to understand and generate human language, making tools like chatbots and translation applications possible. NLP's ability to parse sentiment, handle idiomatic expressions, and develop coherent responses is revolutionary. However, this field also faces significant hurdles, particularly in understanding context and ambiguity. These challenges remind us that while AI can mimic human abilities, it still struggles with the nuances of human interaction.

The comparison between AI and human intelligence has also illuminated the strengths and limitations inherent in each. AI excels in processing large volumes of data and executing repetitive tasks precisely, yet it lacks the emotional depth and intuition defining human thought. This dichotomy presents opportunities for synergy, where the analytical prowess of AI can augment human creativity and decision-making. The potential for collaborative intelligence is immense, promising advancements across various domains as humans and machines work together toward common goals.

As you contemplate these concepts, assess your grasp of the key terms and applications discussed. Consider how AI's strengths and limitations align with your experiences and observations. This reflection will consolidate your understanding and equip you with the confidence to engage in discussions about AI and its role in shaping the future. By embracing this knowledge, you position yourself to navigate the evolving landscape of artificial intelligence with insight and foresight.

As we conclude this initial exploration, take a moment to appreciate the depth and breadth of AI's impact. While the subject is vast and ever-evolving, you have laid a solid foundation for further discovery and application. Understanding AI's fundamental concepts empowers you to think critically about its implications and harness its potential in your own life. As you move forward, remain curious and open to AI's possibilities. The learning journey is ongoing, and each insight gained is a step toward mastering the intricate dance between human and machine intelligence.

2

MANAGING FEAR OF TECHNICAL OBSOLESCENCE: BUSTING AI MYTHS AND LIFELONG LEARNING

Picture this: you're in a crowded coffee shop, savoring your morning brew when your smartphone buzzes with a notification. It's a reminder about an upcoming appointment, scheduled seamlessly through a voice command you issued earlier in the week. As you casually scroll through your favorite online store, you notice that the platform has curated a selection of items tailored to your tastes, thanks to its intuitive recommendation engine. In these moments, artificial intelligence quietly operates in the background of your daily life, enhancing convenience and personalization without demanding your attention. This subtle integration into everyday routines exemplifies how AI has become an essential, yet often overlooked, component of modern existence.

Artificial intelligence isn't confined to futuristic labs or tech conglomerates; it's already deeply embedded in the devices and services we rely upon. Take, for instance, the voice recognition software that powers virtual assistants like Apple's Siri or Amazon's Alexa. These systems employ complex algorithms to interpret and respond to voice commands, transforming ordinary smartphones into powerful tools capable of managing schedules, setting reminders, and even controlling smart home devices. This technology's ability to understand natural language (as described in detail above in the chapter on "natural language processing") and execute tasks exemplifies AI's profound impact on simplifying daily activities.

Another familiar application of AI is online shopping platforms, where recommendation systems analyze user behavior to suggest products that align with individual preferences. Machine learning algorithms achieve a personalization level that scrutinizes past purchases, search queries, and browsing patterns. The benefits are twofold: consumers enjoy a tailored shopping experience, while businesses enhance customer engagement and retention. Such AI-driven systems demonstrate how technology can refine and improve the consumer journey, making it more efficient and enjoyable.

Understanding the role of AI in these contexts not only enriches personal life but also holds significant implications for professional development. AI tools designed to enhance time management and productivity are becoming increasingly common in workplaces. For example, AI-powered scheduling assistants can analyze meeting attendees' availability and preferences, suggesting optimal times to accommodate everyone involved. This automation reduces the back-and-forth often associated with coordinating meetings, freeing valuable time for more critical tasks.

AI applications offer transformative potential in career development by facilitating upskilling and learning. Online platforms leverage AI to recommend courses and resources tailored to an individual's career goals and learning history. This personalized guidance empowers professionals to acquire new skills and stay competitive in an evolving job market. By aligning learning opportunities with career aspirations, AI catalyzes personal and professional growth, enabling individuals to navigate career transitions confidently.

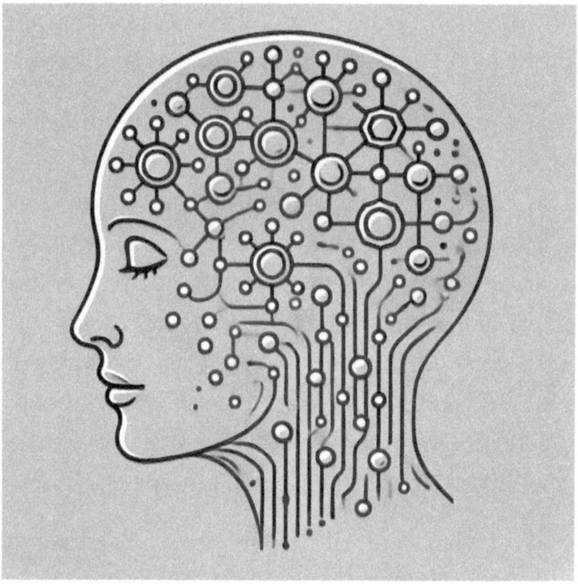

Let's talk about Lila from our Introduction chapter again. She is a finance manager who embraced AI to revolutionize her approach to personal finance management. Faced with the complexity of managing investments, savings, and expenses, Lila turned to an AI-driven financial advisor app. This app analyzed her financial data, offered tailored advice, and even simulated potential investment scenarios. By leveraging AI's analytical capabilities, Lila gained a deeper understanding of her financial health and made informed decisions that aligned with her long-term goals. This example illustrates how AI can empower individuals to take control of their financial future, providing clarity and confidence in managing complex financial landscapes.

The broader impact of AI awareness cannot be overstated. In a world where technology evolves rapidly, understanding AI becomes a vital tool for informed decision-making. AI literacy equips individuals to assess technological advancements critically, differentiating between hype and genuine innovation. This discernment is crucial in an era where new technologies constantly emerge, each promising to reshape industries and societies. Individuals can engage meaningfully in conversations about technology, policy, and ethics by cultivating AI literacy, contributing to a more informed and balanced discourse.

Engaging in societal discussions about AI also enables individuals to play an active role in shaping the future. As AI continues to influence various sectors, from healthcare and finance to education and entertainment, public dialogue becomes essential. Individuals can advocate for ethical AI practices, equitable access to technology, and responsible innovation by participating in these discussions. This engagement fosters a sense of agency and responsibility, emphasizing the importance of collaborative efforts in navigating the digital age.

Exercise for You: Your AI Journey

Consider the AI technologies you interact with regularly, whether they are voice assistants, recommendation systems, or productivity tools. Reflect on how these technologies enhance your daily life and professional endeavors. How do they save time, improve decision-making, or provide personalized experiences? This reflection encourages you to recognize the tangible benefits of AI and consider how a deeper understanding of this technology can further enrich your life.

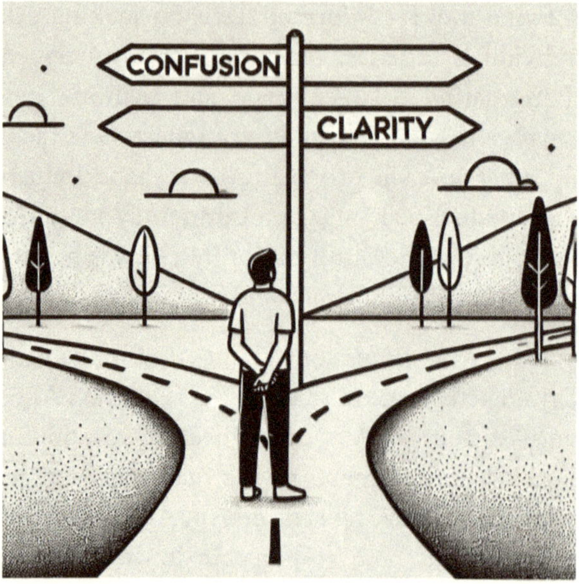

2.1 AI IN THE WORKPLACE: JOB DISPLACEMENT MYTHS

In today's rapidly evolving world, the fear of technological obsolescence is common among many professionals. This anxiety is particularly pronounced regarding artificial intelligence, which is often portrayed as a looming threat to job security. The fear stems from the notion that AI will replace human workers, rendering their skills and expertise redundant. This concern is not unfounded, as AI has transformed industries by automating tasks once performed manually. However, it is crucial to understand that AI is not a monolithic force seeking to replace humans but a tool designed to augment human capabilities and enhance productivity.

The fear of job loss and economic displacement is the most pervasive myth surrounding AI. It is essential to recognize that while AI can automate specific tasks, it also creates new opportunities for innovation and growth. Integrating AI into various sectors has led to the emergence of new roles and industries, with a demand for professionals skilled in managing and maintaining AI systems. Human oversight remains indispensable in AI development, as machines rely on human input to function effectively. AI systems are designed by humans, for humans, and their success depends on the creativity, intuition, and ethical considerations that only humans can provide.

AI's capabilities are impressive, but they are not without limitations. While AI excels at processing vast amounts of data and identifying patterns, it lacks the creative and emotional intelligence that humans possess. Machines can analyze data and generate insights but cannot replicate the nuanced understanding and empathy humans bring to complex situations. This limitation underscores the importance of human involvement in AI development and deployment. AI systems require human oversight to align with ethical standards and societal values. Machines must be programmed and monitored by humans to prevent biases and errors arising from flawed algorithms or incomplete data.

Evidence and expert opinions are essential to dispel common myths about AI. Studies have shown that AI is more likely to complement human work than to replace it entirely. Experts emphasize that AI systems are designed to work within specific parameters and require human guidance to operate effectively. AI is not fully autonomous; it depends on human input and collaboration to achieve its full potential. By highlighting these insights, we can demystify AI and alleviate fears about its impact on the workforce.

AI's role in job transformation is significant. By automating routine tasks, AI frees up time for employees to engage in higher-value activities, fostering innovation and creativity. This shift enhances job satisfaction and boosts productivity, as workers can devote their energy to tasks that require human judgment and insight. For example, in data entry roles, AI can handle the monotonous task of data input, allowing employees to analyze and interpret the data instead. Additionally, AI is giving rise to new roles focusing on managing and overseeing these technologies. Positions such as AI trainers, ethicists, and data analysts are emerging, requiring new skills and offering new career opportunities. Thus, AI is expanding and diversifying its roles and responsibilities rather than diminishing the workforce.

Consider the integration of AI in manufacturing through collaborative robots, or cobots, which work alongside human operators. These machines handle repetitive and physically demanding tasks, such as assembly line work, reducing the risk of injury and fatigue for human workers. Cobots enhance productivity and efficiency while allowing human workers to focus on tasks that require dexterity and problem-solving skills. AI augments human capabilities in customer service by managing routine inquiries through chatbots, leaving complex customer issues to human agents. This collaboration ensures that customers receive timely assistance while allowing human agents to handle more nuanced interactions that benefit from a personal touch. These examples demonstrate how AI and human workers coexist harmoniously, complementing each other's capabilities to achieve better outcomes.

2.2 AI AND LIFELONG LEARNING: ADAPTING TO AN AI-ENHANCED WORKPLACE

Remaining relevant in an AI-driven world requires continuous learning and adaptability. As technology continues to evolve, professionals must embrace lifelong learning as a strategy for career resilience. This lifelong learning involves staying informed about AI advancements, acquiring new skills, and adapting to changing industry demands. Focusing on uniquely human skills, such as creativity, empathy, and critical thinking, can also provide a competitive edge in the job market. These skills are difficult for machines to replicate, making them valuable assets in an AI-enhanced workplace.

Success stories abound of individuals and organizations that have successfully adapted to AI advancements. Consider a company that has integrated AI into its operations while preserving human jobs. By automating repetitive tasks, the company frees up employees to focus on higher-value activities that require human judgment and creativity. This approach enhances productivity and fosters a culture of innovation and collaboration. Similarly, professionals who have harnessed AI to improve their skill sets find themselves better equipped to navigate the evolving landscape of their industries. By embracing AI as a tool for growth, they position themselves to thrive in an increasingly digital world.

As the demand for AI-related skills grows, upskilling and reskilling initiatives become vital strategies for staying relevant in the workforce. Employees are encouraged to engage in ongoing education through formal training programs, online courses, or workshops. This proactive approach to learning empowers workers to acquire new competencies, positioning them to take on roles that require specialized knowledge and expertise. Lifelong learning emerges as a strategy for career resilience, enabling individuals to navigate the evolving job market confidently. By embracing this mindset, workers can transform potential challenges AI poses into opportunities for personal and professional growth.

The work landscape is shifting, driven by technological advancements that redefine what it means to be productive and innovative. While concerns about AI-induced job loss persist, they are largely overshadowed by the potential for AI to complement human effort, creating a more efficient and dynamic workplace. As industries adapt to these changes, the focus shifts from fear of obsolescence to embracing AI's possibilities. By fostering an environment that encourages learning and adaptation, businesses can harness the full potential of AI while empowering their workforce to thrive in this new era of work. The role of AI is not to replace human workers but to enhance their capabilities, leading to a future where technology and humanity work together to achieve shared goals.

Chapter 2 Self-Assessment

Reflecting on how artificial intelligence fits into your life and career can be enlightening and empowering. Considering how AI intersects with your daily activities, think about the technology you interact with most frequently. The automated systems at your workplace or the smart devices at home simplify everyday tasks. These interactions are often seamless, yet they signify a more significant trend of AI integration into our personal and professional spheres. Such reflection can deepen your understanding of AI's pervasive role and highlight areas where you might enhance your knowledge or skills.

AI might influence how you work in your career, even if subtly. Whether you know it or not, AI technologies are transforming industries by automating routine tasks and providing data-driven insights that inform decision-making. Consider the tools and systems you use that rely on AI. Do they streamline processes, improve accuracy, or offer new capabilities previously unavailable? By identifying these contributions, you can assess how AI enhances productivity and efficiency in your field and where there might be opportunities for further application or innovation.

Understanding AI myths and fears is crucial in addressing concerns about technological obsolescence. It's easy to feel apprehensive about the rapid pace of AI development, mainly when headlines often focus on potential job losses or ethical dilemmas. However, separating fact from fiction allows for a more balanced perspective. AI is designed to augment human abilities, not render them obsolete. It requires human creativity and oversight to function effectively. By debunking myths, you can better appreciate AI's potential benefits and identify ways to leverage it for personal and professional growth.

Consider also the strategies you might adopt to remain relevant in an AI-driven world. Continuous learning is paramount, enabling you to adapt to technological advancements and keeping your skills current. Think about the areas where you might expand your knowledge or develop new competencies, which could involve learning about AI-related technologies or focusing on uniquely human skills that machines cannot easily replicate, such as critical thinking, creativity, and emotional intelligence. By cultivating these skills, you enhance your ability to collaborate with AI systems and navigate the evolving job market.

Reflect on the success stories you've encountered about individuals or organizations adapting to AI advancements. These narratives can offer valuable insights into practical strategies for integration and adaptation. Whether it's a company that has successfully incorporated AI into its operations while maintaining human jobs or professionals who have used AI to augment their expertise, these examples illustrate the potential for positive outcomes. They also highlight the importance of a proactive approach to AI adoption, where individuals and organizations actively seek ways to benefit from technological innovations.

As you conclude your self-assessment, recognize that understanding AI is an ongoing process. The reflections you've explored here serve as a foundation for deeper engagement with AI and its potential applications. By staying curious and open to new possibilities, you can actively shape your relationship with AI and leverage it to navigate the evolving professional landscape.

This chapter has examined the opportunities and challenges presented by AI, encouraging thoughtful reflection on its role in everyday life and career development. As we transition into the next chapter, we will shift our focus to real-world applications of AI—exploring how this technology is being actively used across industries and how you can take practical steps to integrate it into your work and life.

3

REAL-WORLD APPLICATIONS OF AI

In this chapter, I want to share responses to questions about how AI transforms various industries and personal productivity. What is AI´s role in entertainment, curating content, enhancing creativity, and personal productivity, where intelligent assistants and automation tools streamline daily tasks? What is AI´s impact on healthcare, revolutionizing patient care and medical research? What is AI´s role in retail, and where is it reshaping shopping experiences? What is AI's influence in finance, improving fraud detection and financial planning, and in education, where it personalizes learning experiences?

By the end of this chapter, you will have a broader understanding of AI's practical, real-world applications and the opportunity to reflect on how these innovations could impact your life and career. Let's dive into the ways AI is shaping the world around us.

3.1 AI IN ENTERTAINMENT: REDEFINING AUDIENCE ENGAGEMENT AND CREATIVITY

After a long day, you might settle into your living room, ready to unwind with your favorite show, and find your streaming service presenting personalized recommendations tailored to your preferences. Sophisticated artificial intelligence algorithms power this seemingly straightforward experience. AI's impact on the entertainment industry extends far beyond what is immediately noticeable, influencing everything from content curation to the creation of innovative media formats. Through your interactions with these platforms, you continuously engage with AI, enriching your viewing, listening, and interactive experiences—often without even realizing its transformative role.

AI's role in personalizing user experiences, particularly entertainment, is profound and pervasive. Take Netflix, for instance, which uses AI to analyze viewing habits and predict what you might want to watch next. By examining your past interactions, such as the genres you favor or the patterns in your viewing times, Netflix's recommendation engine curates a tailored list of suggestions. This personalization improves your experience by reducing decision fatigue and increases engagement with the platform, as you're more likely to find content that resonates with you. Similarly, Spotify employs AI through its Discover Weekly feature, which curates playlists based on your listening history. By identifying patterns in your preferences and those of similar users, Spotify delivers a personalized musical journey each week, enhancing your connection to the service and introducing you to new artists and genres you might otherwise overlook.

Beyond user experience, AI significantly contributes to content creation within the entertainment sector. Generative AI technologies can now compose original music, blending various styles and influences to produce new compositions. These AI-generated pieces can serve as the foundation for artists seeking inspiration or looking to explore novel musical territories. In film and television, AI assists scriptwriters by suggesting plot developments, character arcs, or dialogue options, offering a new layer of creativity and efficiency in the storytelling process. By using AI to streamline and enhance these creative tasks, content creators can focus more on the artistic elements of their work while AI handles more technical or repetitive aspects.

The gaming industry also benefits immensely from AI's capabilities, particularly in crafting immersive and dynamic experiences. AI is pivotal in developing adaptive difficulty levels that respond to player performance. This ensures that games remain challenging yet enjoyable, catering to novices and seasoned players. AI also breathes life into non-player characters, enabling them to exhibit realistic behaviors and interactions. These characters can adapt to player actions, creating more engaging and unpredictable scenarios that enhance the gaming experience. As AI continues to evolve, its influence in gaming is likely to expand, offering even more personalized and interactive environments.

Emerging AI technologies promise to further transform entertainment, mainly through virtual reality (VR) advancements. AI's integration into VR can lead to experiences that are not only visually immersive but also dynamically responsive to user interactions. Imagine a VR narrative that adapts based on your decisions in real-time, offering a unique story with each playthrough. AI-driven interactive storytelling can revolutionize how narratives are constructed and experienced, allowing for a more engaging and personalized approach to storytelling. As these technologies mature, the line between audience and participant blurs, inviting you to become an active creator in the stories you consume.

Exercise for You: AI's Influence on Your Entertainment Choices

Consider the last time you engaged with an entertainment platform—streaming a movie, listening to music, or playing a video game. Reflect on how AI might have influenced your experience, from personalized recommendations to adaptive gameplay. How did these AI-driven elements enhance your interaction? This reflection encourages you to recognize the subtle yet significant ways AI enriches your entertainment experiences, making them more tailored and enjoyable.

3.2 AI FOR PERSONAL PRODUCTIVITY: ORGANIZING YOUR LIFE

Managing time and tasks effectively can often feel overwhelming in the fast-paced rhythm of our lives. Fortunately, AI-powered productivity tools transform how you organize your life, providing innovative solutions to streamline and optimize daily routines. Take intelligent scheduling assistants such as Google Calendar, which utilizes AI to suggest meeting times based on participants' availability and preferences. Analyzing patterns in your schedule proposes optimal times for appointments, reducing the back-and-forth typically involved in setting up meetings. This intelligent scheduling saves you time and enhances efficiency by ensuring your calendar aligns seamlessly with your commitments and priorities.

Task management is another area where AI significantly enhances productivity by automating and prioritizing tasks. Consider AI-driven to-do list applications that can learn from your habits and preferences, helping you manage tasks more effectively. These apps can suggest which tasks to tackle based on deadlines, importance, and urgency, allowing you to focus on what truly matters. Additionally, machine learning algorithms in email clients can sort and prioritize your inbox, filtering out spam and highlighting essential messages. This capability enables you to easily manage your communications, ensuring critical emails receive your attention promptly while you can relegate less important ones to the background.

Communication, a cornerstone of productivity, also benefits from AI's advancements. Tools like Grammarly employ sophisticated AI algorithms to enhance your writing by identifying grammatical errors, suggesting stylistic improvements, and ensuring clarity. Whether drafting an email or composing a report, AI-assisted writing tools provide real-time feedback, elevating the quality of your communication. Furthermore, real-time language translation services break down language barriers, facilitating seamless communication across different languages. Whether collaborating with international colleagues or traveling abroad, these services ensure that language differences do not impede your interactions.

The future holds even more promise for AI-driven productivity enhancements. Imagine AI forecasting tools that assist in project management by predicting potential bottlenecks and resource constraints. These tools could analyze project timelines, resource allocations, and historical data to provide insights that help you make informed decisions. Additionally, voice-activated personal assistants continue to evolve, offering more seamless task execution. These assistants can manage tasks using voice commands, from setting reminders to booking flights, allowing you to multitask without breaking your workflow. As AI technology advances, the potential for further optimizing personal and professional productivity grows exponentially, promising more intuitive tools integrated into your daily life.

3.3 AI IN HEALTHCARE: TRANSFORMING PATIENT CARE

In healthcare, artificial intelligence is reshaping the landscape of patient care and medical diagnostics, offering unprecedented accuracy and efficiency. AI-powered imaging systems have revolutionized early disease detection, allowing healthcare professionals to identify conditions such as cancer or cardiovascular disease at stages when they are most treatable. These systems analyze medical images with a precision that rivals human radiologists, detecting anomalies that otherwise might be overlooked. By integrating AI into radiology, patients benefit from faster diagnoses, which can significantly improve treatment outcomes. Furthermore, AI enhances treatment planning through predictive analytics, providing personalized treatment plans tailored to individual patient profiles. By examining vast datasets of patient histories and treatment outcomes, AI models predict the most effective interventions, streamlining decision-making for healthcare providers and optimizing patient care.

Beyond diagnostics, AI is crucial in real-time patient monitoring, offering a continuous stream of data that informs proactive healthcare management. Wearable devices with AI-driven sensors track vital signs such as heart rate, blood pressure, and oxygen levels, transmitting this data to healthcare providers in real-time. These devices serve as an early warning system, alerting medical teams to potential health issues before they escalate into critical emergencies. For instance, an AI algorithm might detect subtle changes in a patient's heart rhythm, prompting a timely intervention that could prevent a heart attack. This level of monitoring empowers patients to take charge of their health while enabling providers to deliver timely, responsive care, reducing the burden on healthcare systems and improving patient outcomes.

AI's transformative impact extends to drug discovery, expediting the development of new medications with remarkable speed. Traditional drug discovery is a lengthy, costly process, often taking years to bring a new drug to market. However, AI models accelerate this timeline by predicting drug interactions and their efficacy, narrowing down potential compounds for further testing. By simulating how different molecules interact within the human body, AI can identify promising candidates for clinical trials, reducing the time and cost associated with drug development. This capability not only hastens the availability of new treatments but also opens avenues for personalized medicine, where therapies are tailored to an individual patient's genetic and biochemical makeup.

However, the integration of AI in healthcare is not without ethical considerations, raising important questions about patient data privacy and the role of AI in decision-making. AI relies heavily on access to large volumes of patient data, leading to concerns about the security and confidentiality of sensitive information. Ensuring robust data protection measures is paramount to maintaining patient trust and compliance with privacy regulations. Moreover, as AI systems increasingly influence medical decisions, questions arise regarding accountability and the potential for algorithmic bias. Healthcare institutions need to implement transparent and ethical AI practices, ensuring that AI can augment human expertise rather than replace it. By fostering collaboration between technology developers, healthcare professionals, and regulatory bodies, the ethical challenges of AI can be navigated effectively, paving the way for a future where AI enhances, rather than compromises, the quality of patient care.

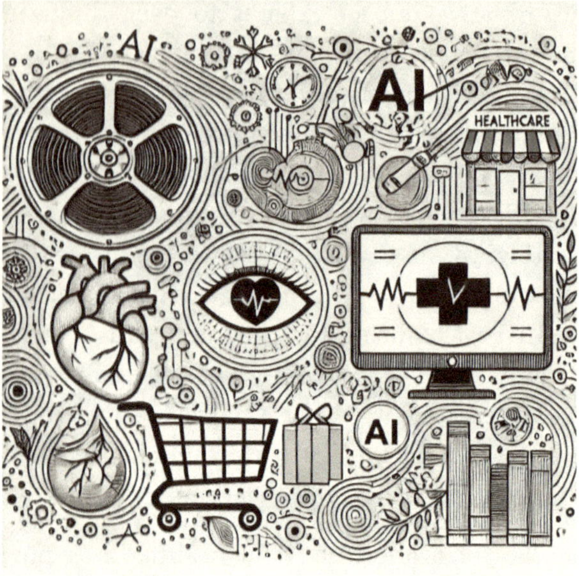

3.4 AI IN RETAIL: ENHANCING SHOPPING EXPERIENCES

When you browse an online store, the product array is not accidental. Behind the scenes, artificial intelligence works diligently to personalize your shopping experience, tailoring it to your unique preferences and past behaviors. Sophisticated algorithms achieve a personalization level that analyzes your browsing history, purchase patterns, and even the frequency of your visits. By processing this data, AI can predict what items you might be interested in, curating a selection of products that align with your tastes. This approach is beneficial for consumers, who find products more quickly, and also advantageous for retailers, who see improved customer satisfaction and loyalty. The result is a shopping experience that feels intuitive and personalized as if the store knows just what you need before you even realize it.

Beyond personalization, AI revolutionizes the management of retail inventories, optimizing supply chain processes in ways that were previously unimaginable. Demand forecasting, a critical inventory management component, has been transformed by AI's ability to analyze large datasets precisely. Retailers can now anticipate consumer demand more accurately, adjusting their stock levels accordingly to avoid shortages and surpluses. Automated restocking systems further enhance this efficiency by replenishing shelves promptly when inventory levels drop below a certain threshold. This automation reduces human error and labor costs, allowing retailers to maintain optimal stock levels with minimal oversight. Integrating AI into supply chain operations results in a more efficient retail ecosystem, where resources are allocated judiciously, and waste is minimized.

Customer service, a cornerstone of retail, has also transformed through the application of AI technologies. Chatbots, for instance, provide 24/7 assistance to customers, handling inquiries and solving problems quickly and accurately. These AI-driven virtual assistants can manage various tasks, from answering common questions to processing orders and returns. By employing natural language processing and sentiment analysis, chatbots can understand and respond to customer emotions, ensuring that interactions remain empathetic and practical. This level of service ensures that customers receive the support they need anytime, enhancing their overall experience and fostering loyalty. Moreover, AI's ability to analyze customer feedback provides valuable insights into consumer preferences and pain points, enabling retailers to continuously refine their offerings and improve satisfaction.

Looking to the future, AI promises even more innovative solutions that will further enhance retail experiences. Imagine walking into a store where augmented reality fitting rooms allow you to try on clothes virtually, assessing fit and style without needing physical garments. This technology, powered by AI, could revolutionize how we shop for clothing, offering convenience and reducing the need for extensive inventories. Similarly, AI-powered cashier-less stores are on the horizon, where you can pick up items and walk out, with transactions completed seamlessly through AI systems that track your selections in real-time. These advancements promise to streamline shopping experiences and redefine the nature of retail environments, making them more interactive, efficient, and aligned with consumer expectations. Integrating AI into retail is not just a trend but a transformative force that continues to reshape the industry, offering new possibilities for retailers and consumers alike.

3.5 AI IN FINANCE: SMARTER INVESTMENTS

In the complex world of finance, artificial intelligence is emerging as a powerful force that is reshaping investment strategies and financial analysis. At the heart of this transformation is AI's ability to process vast amounts of data quickly and accurately, providing previously unattainable insights. Consider the role of AI algorithms in predicting stock market movements. These algorithms analyze market trends, historical data, and economic indicators to anticipate shifts in stock prices, enabling investors to make informed decisions. By identifying patterns and anomalies that might elude human analysts, AI enhances the precision of investment decisions, offering a competitive edge in the dynamic landscape of financial markets.

Beyond investment analysis, AI safeguards financial transactions through advanced fraud detection mechanisms. Real-time transaction monitoring systems powered by AI continuously scan for suspicious activities, flagging potential threats before they escalate. These systems utilize pattern recognition to detect anomalies that might indicate fraudulent behavior, such as unusual spending patterns or unauthorized access attempts. By swiftly identifying and addressing potential fraud, AI helps financial institutions protect their client's assets and maintain trust in their services. This capability is especially vital in an era where digital transactions are rampant and cyber threats are an ever-present concern.

AI's influence extends to personal finance, which empowers individuals to manage their financial health more quickly and efficiently. AI-driven budgeting apps provide insights into spending habits, helping users track expenses, set savings goals, and optimize their budgets. These apps analyze transaction data to offer personalized recommendations, encouraging more disciplined financial behavior. Additionally, AI-powered financial advice services provide customized investment strategies tailored to individual risk profiles and financial goals. These services provide actionable insights that guide users toward achieving monetary stability and growth by considering income, expenses, and long-term objectives.

Looking to the future, AI promises to revolutionize financial services further with innovations that could reshape how investments are managed and transactions are conducted. One such advancement is the rise of AI-based robo-advisors, which offer automated portfolio management services. These digital platforms assess an individual's financial situation and investment preferences, creating and managing a diversified portfolio with minimal human intervention. By leveraging AI's analytical capabilities, robo-advisors provide cost-effective investment solutions accessible to a broader audience. Moreover, combining blockchain technology and AI unlocks exciting possibilities for secure transactions. Blockchain's decentralized ledger system and AI's data processing power could enhance transparency and reduce fraud, offering a more secure and efficient framework for financial transactions.

As AI continues to permeate the finance sector, it redefines traditional practices and opens new avenues for innovation. The integration of AI in financial analysis, fraud detection, and personal finance management has already demonstrated its potential to enhance accuracy, efficiency, and accessibility. As these technologies evolve, they promise to deliver even more significant benefits, empowering institutions and individuals to navigate the financial landscape with confidence and foresight.

3.6 AI IN EDUCATION: PERSONALIZED LEARNING PATHS

Artificial intelligence is transforming education by tailoring learning experiences to meet the unique needs of each student. Gone are the days when education followed a one-size-fits-all model. Today, adaptive learning platforms use AI to assess students' strengths and weaknesses, dynamically adjusting content difficulty to provide an optimal learning experience. This personalization ensures that each learner progresses at their own pace, fostering a deeper understanding of the material. For instance, if a student struggles with a particular math concept, the system can present additional exercises or alternative explanations until the student achieves mastery. Conversely, if students excel, the platform can introduce more challenging material to keep them engaged. This approach enhances learning outcomes and boosts student confidence and motivation.

AI's impact extends beyond the classroom, streamlining administrative tasks that traditionally consume significant time and resources. Automated grading systems provide immediate feedback on assignments, freeing educators from the manual grading process and allowing them to focus on more meaningful interactions with students. These systems use machine learning algorithms to evaluate written assignments, quizzes, and complex assessments, identifying patterns and providing constructive feedback. Furthermore, AI-driven enrollment and scheduling tools optimize administrative efficiency by managing student registrations, course assignments, and timetable creation. By automating these processes, educational institutions can allocate resources more effectively and provide a smoother experience for both students and staff.

In skill development, AI is at the forefront of fostering new competencies that prepare students for the demands of the modern workforce. AI-powered language learning applications offer personalized lessons that adapt to the learner's pace and proficiency level. These apps utilize speech recognition and natural language processing to provide real-time feedback on pronunciation and grammar, facilitating language acquisition more interactively and engagingly. Additionally, virtual labs for science and technology education simulate real-world scenarios, allowing students to experiment and explore without the constraints of physical resources. These labs provide hands-on experiences that enhance understanding and retention, preparing students for careers in STEM fields.

Looking to the future, AI promises to bring even more advancements to the educational landscape, potentially revolutionizing how we learn and teach. Imagine classrooms where virtual reality environments bring historical events to life, or AI tutors provide personalized support to each student, regardless of location. AI could enable educators to develop customized curricula that reflect individual learning styles and interests, fostering a more inclusive and equitable educational environment. Additionally, AI's ability to analyze educational data on a large scale could provide insights into effective teaching strategies and learning outcomes, driving continuous improvement in educational practices. As AI continues to evolve, its role in shaping the future of education will undoubtedly expand, creating opportunities for more personalized, engaging, and effective learning experiences for all students.

Chapter 3 Self-Assessment

Reflecting on the transformative power of artificial intelligence across various industries offers an opportunity to appreciate its profound impact on personal and professional realms. This chapter has explored the multifaceted applications of AI, demonstrating how it enhances everyday experiences and revolutionizes business operations. From entertainment to healthcare and beyond, AI's integration reshapes how we interact with technology, offering personalized, efficient, and innovative solutions to longstanding challenges.

In the entertainment industry, AI has emerged as a catalyst for personalized experiences, enabling platforms to curate content that resonates with individual preferences. Whether suggesting new films or crafting playlists that align with your musical tastes, AI ensures your media engagement is intuitive and enjoyable. The seamless integration of AI in these platforms enhances user satisfaction and drives engagement and loyalty, illustrating the symbiotic relationship between technology and consumer behavior.

As we transition to personal productivity, AI plays a pivotal role in streamlining daily tasks and optimizing workflows. AI-driven tools have transformed how we manage time, prioritize tasks, and communicate effectively. These innovations, rooted in sophisticated algorithms and machine learning, offer solutions that adapt to our unique needs, providing a personalized approach to productivity that was once unimaginable. By automating routine tasks and offering insights into our habits,

AI empowers us to focus on what truly matters, enhancing efficiency and effectiveness.

Healthcare, too, has experienced a paradigm shift with the integration of AI technologies. The precision and speed offered by AI in diagnostics and treatment planning are revolutionizing patient care, enabling healthcare providers to deliver more accurate and timely interventions. AI's ability to analyze vast datasets and identify patterns that may elude human practitioners underscores its potential to improve outcomes and streamline operations. As AI continues to evolve, its role in healthcare promises to expand, offering new opportunities for innovation and improved patient experiences.

In retail, AI transforms the shopping experience, bringing consumers a new level of personalization and efficiency. From inventory management to customer service, AI-driven solutions optimize operations and enhance customer satisfaction. By predicting consumer behavior and adapting to real-time data, retailers can offer tailored experiences that cater to individual preferences, fostering loyalty and engagement. The integration of AI in retail reflects a broader trend towards more responsive and dynamic business models, where technology plays a crucial role in shaping consumer interactions.

The finance sector, with its complex landscape, has also embraced AI to enhance decision-making and safeguard transactions. The insights provided by AI in financial analysis and fraud detection offer a layer of security and precision that is invaluable in today's digital economy. These advancements protect assets and empower individuals to manage their finances with greater confidence and control. As AI continues to develop, its potential to reshape financial services is immense, promising more accessible and personalized solutions for consumers.

Education, a cornerstone of societal development, is witnessing a transformation through AI's ability to personalize learning experiences and streamline administrative processes. The adaptability of AI-driven platforms ensures that educational content meets students' diverse needs, fostering a more inclusive and effective learning environment. By automating routine tasks and offering insights into student performance, AI supports educators in their mission to cultivate knowledge and skills, preparing the next generation for the challenges and opportunities of the future.

As you reflect on these themes, consider how AI's integration into these sectors enhances your daily life and the broader societal landscape. The innovations discussed in this chapter highlight AI's potential to drive progress and underscore the importance of understanding and engaging with this technology. Recognizing AI's impact allows you to navigate an increasingly digital world with insight and foresight. As we move forward, the exploration of AI's applications will continue to reveal new possibilities, inviting us to reimagine the future of technology and its role in our lives.

4

ETHICAL AND SOCIETAL IMPLICATIONS OF AI

You enter a job interview feeling optimistic about the opportunity ahead, yet as you greet your interviewer, you may unknowingly interact with decisions already influenced by artificial intelligence. AI systems increasingly shape significant aspects of our lives—from hiring processes to financial approvals. This expanding reliance on technology highlights critical concerns about fairness and bias, especially when algorithms carry hidden prejudices capable of subtly but significantly affecting outcomes. As AI further integrates into decision-making, recognizing and addressing its ethical implications is essential for promoting societal equity and fairness.

Fairness in AI ensures that systems treat all individuals equitably, without favor or prejudice. It's about creating algorithms that do not discriminate against any group, reflecting the diversity and inclusivity we strive for in society. Bias, on the other hand, represents the systematic favoritism of certain groups over others. It can manifest when AI systems produce outcomes that disadvantage specific demographics, often because of underlying data or design flaws. Bias can inadvertently perpetuate societal inequalities, reinforcing stereotypes and creating barriers to opportunity for marginalized groups. Understanding these concepts is essential for developing AI systems that uphold ethical standards and serve the broader good.

Bias in AI often originates from the data used to train these systems. Training data that reflects societal prejudices can lead to biased outcomes, as AI models learn from the patterns in the data they are exposed to. If a dataset is skewed towards a particular demographic, the resulting AI system may not perform equally well across different groups. For example, facial recognition systems often exhibit higher error rates for minority groups than their performance with majority populations. This disparity can be traced back to training datasets lacking diversity and failing to represent all segments of society adequately. Algorithmic biases can also arise from flawed design choices, where the assumptions and decisions made during the development process inadvertently favor specific outcomes over others.

Real-world examples of AI bias underscore the importance of vigilance and corrective action. In recruitment, algorithms designed to streamline hiring can inadvertently favor candidates from specific backgrounds if the training data reflects historical hiring biases. Amazon's now-abandoned hiring tool, which favored male-associated terms, exemplifies this issue. Such biases can perpetuate workplace inequalities, limiting diversity and stifling innovation. Similarly, online advertising platforms often display high-paying job ads more frequently to men than women, highlighting the need for greater scrutiny in algorithmic decision-making. These examples illustrate the tangible impact of bias and the importance of addressing it proactively to ensure fairness and equality in AI applications.

Mitigating bias in AI systems requires a multifaceted approach, beginning with the data itself. Ensuring diverse and representative datasets is a foundational step in reducing bias. AI models can learn to perform equitably across different groups by including data from varied demographics. Regular audits and impact assessments of AI models are also crucial for identifying and addressing biases that may arise over time. These evaluations help maintain the integrity of AI systems, ensuring they continue to meet ethical standards and serve their intended purpose. Institutions like IBM emphasize the importance of AI governance, advocating for practices that promote trust, transparency, fairness, and human oversight to responsibly guide the development and deployment of AI technologies.

Exercise for You: Examining Fairness and Bias in Everyday AI

Consider the AI systems you encounter daily, from social media algorithms to online shopping recommendations. Reflect on how these systems might influence your decisions and interactions. Do you notice any patterns or biases in how they operate? This reflection encourages you to think critically about the role of AI in shaping your experiences and the importance of advocating for fairness and transparency in its applications.

Understanding their ethical implications becomes increasingly essential as you continue to engage with AI technologies. By recognizing the potential for bias and taking steps to mitigate it, you contribute to a more equitable and just society. This chapter explores these themes in depth, offering insights into how we can navigate the complexities of AI with integrity and foresight.

4.1 PRIVACY CONCERNS: PROTECTING PERSONAL DATA

In today's AI-driven world, data is the most valuable asset, shaping everything from decisions to innovations. It fuels the algorithms that power AI systems, driving innovations that reshape industries and redefine interactions. As you navigate this digital landscape, your data becomes a valuable resource sought after by companies eager to refine their AI models. This data, from browsing habits to purchase histories, enriches AI systems, enabling them to deliver personalized experiences. However, this reliance on personal data also raises significant privacy concerns, as the potential misuse of information looms large. Understanding the importance of data privacy is crucial, as it safeguards against the intrusive surveillance and exploitation that can arise when personal information is mishandled.

While the benefits of AI are manifold, the risks to personal data privacy are equally pressing. When you engage with digital platforms, you may unknowingly consent to collecting and monitoring your data. This unconsented data gathering often occurs without explicit permission, leading to a sense of unease about who has access to your information and how it might be used. Beyond the initial collection, the danger of data breaches further exacerbates privacy concerns. A single breach can expose sensitive data to malicious actors, resulting in identity theft, financial loss, and reputational damage. These risks underscore the necessity for robust data protection measures, mainly as AI systems increasingly rely on vast amounts of personal information to function effectively.

Legal and regulatory frameworks have been established to protect data privacy. The General Data Protection Regulation (GDPR), implemented by the European Union, serves as a cornerstone. GDPR enforces strict guidelines on data protection, emphasizing transparency, user consent, and the right to access personal data. It has set a global benchmark, inspiring similar legislation in other regions. The California Consumer Privacy Act (CCPA) mirrors GDPR's principles in the United States, granting consumers greater control over their personal information. These laws empower individuals by mandating that companies disclose data collection practices and respect consumer rights. As privacy legislation evolves, it becomes a pivotal tool in safeguarding personal data and ensuring that AI's advancements do not come at the expense of individual privacy.

Beyond legal frameworks, best practices in data privacy offer additional layers of protection. Ensuring data remains secure begins with encryption, a process that scrambles information, making it unreadable to unauthorized users. This fundamental step prevents potential breaches from exposing sensitive data. Secure data storage further enhances protection by keeping information in safe environments through cloud services with robust security protocols or localized storage solutions. Transparency in data practices plays a critical role as well. Organizations build trust with users by clearly communicating how data is collected, used, and shared, fostering a culture of openness and accountability. This transparency reassures individuals that their data is handled responsibly, reducing fears of misuse.

As you navigate the digital ecosystem, adopting personal data privacy practices empowers you to take control of your information. Being discerning about the permissions you grant apps and services is vital. Limiting data sharing to what is necessary minimizes exposure and reduces the risk of exploitation. Reviewing privacy settings on digital platforms ensures that they align with your preferences and comfort levels. Educating yourself about data privacy rights and staying informed about new regulations equips you with the knowledge to advocate for your privacy effectively. By actively engaging in these practices, you contribute to a digital environment where privacy is respected and protected.

Data privacy remains crucial as AI continues to evolve and permeate everyday life. The balance between leveraging personal data for AI advancements and protecting individual privacy is delicate, requiring vigilance and proactive measures. As you embrace AI's conveniences, understanding and prioritizing data privacy ensures that these technologies enhance your life without compromising your rights. The ongoing dialogue surrounding data privacy reflects society's commitment to navigating this complex landscape, striving to find harmony between technological progress and preserving personal freedoms.

4.2 AI AND SOCIETY: SHAPING THE FUTURE

Artificial intelligence stands on the brink of redefining society as we know it, promising to address some of the most pressing global challenges. Consider climate change, a threat that looms large over our planet. AI offers innovative solutions to mitigate its effects, from optimizing energy consumption in smart grids to predicting weather patterns with unprecedented accuracy. By analyzing vast datasets, AI systems can identify trends and propose actionable strategies to reduce carbon footprints. These advancements enhance our understanding of climate dynamics and empower policy-makers to make informed decisions that benefit the environment.

In healthcare, AI's potential to improve accessibility is equally remarkable. Imagine a world where AI-driven diagnostics enable remote areas to access quality medical care. Through AI-powered telemedicine platforms, patients can receive accurate assessments without needing to travel, bridging the gap between urban and rural healthcare access. AI algorithms analyze medical images and data, providing insights that enhance diagnosis and treatment options. Such advancements promise to democratize healthcare, ensuring that quality care is no longer confined to those with geographical or financial advantages.

However, deploying AI technologies brings with it a host of ethical dilemmas. Balancing the drive for innovation with ethical considerations is a challenge that society must navigate carefully. The rapid pace of AI advancement often outstrips the development of moral frameworks, raising questions about accountability and transparency. As AI systems increasingly make decisions that impact human lives, ensuring that these technologies align with societal values becomes paramount. This involves creating robust ethical guidelines and engaging in dialogues addressing AI deployment's potential consequences.

AI's influence extends beyond technological applications, profoundly affecting social dynamics. The rise of AI-powered platforms has revolutionized online communication and social media, changing how we interact and share information. Algorithms curate content, shaping the narratives and information that reach users. While this personalization enhances user experience, it also poses risks by creating echo chambers that reinforce biases and limit exposure to diverse perspectives. Furthermore, AI-driven surveillance technologies impact privacy and personal autonomy, prompting debates about the balance between security and individual rights.

Speculating on future AI developments reveals a landscape rich with possibilities. Autonomous vehicles, once the realm of science fiction, are becoming a reality, promising to transform transportation systems and urban planning. These vehicles, equipped with AI, can optimize traffic flow, reduce accidents, and lower emissions. As cities evolve into innovative environments, AI will play a key role in managing resources efficiently, from energy consumption to waste management. The concept of smart cities, where interconnected systems enhance the quality of life, is increasingly within reach.

In governance, AI-enhanced decision-making can revolutionize how policies are crafted and implemented. AI can identify patterns and predict outcomes by analyzing vast amounts of data, informing more effective and equitable policy decisions. This capability allows governments to respond proactively to societal challenges, from healthcare crises to economic fluctuations. However, integrating AI into governance also demands careful consideration of privacy, bias, and the human touch, which are essential for truly understanding complex social issues.

As AI continues to shape the future, its implications for society are vast and multifaceted. The potential to address global challenges, enhance healthcare, and transform social dynamics is immense, yet these advancements must be pursued with thoughtfulness and responsibility. Embracing AI's possibilities requires a commitment to ethical innovation, ensuring that technology serves humanity's best interests. The path forward is one of exploration and adaptation, where society must navigate the complexities of AI's role in shaping a connected and conscious world.

4.3 RESPONSIBLE AI USE: BEST PRACTICES

In the evolving landscape of artificial intelligence, the call for responsible AI use has never been more pertinent. This concept revolves around the principles of ethical development and deployment of AI technologies, ensuring that they align with human values and societal norms. At its core, responsible AI use is about prioritizing ethical considerations throughout the lifecycle of AI projects. This involves the technical aspects and moral and social implications of AI applications. Developers and organizations must ensure that their AI systems operate transparently and fairly, minimizing harm and maximizing benefits for all stakeholders. By focusing on ethical guidelines, responsible AI use seeks to cultivate trust and accountability, reinforcing that technology should serve humanity rather than undermine it.

A key component of responsible AI is the establishment of best practices that guide ethical AI implementation. Transparency in AI algorithms and decision-making processes is essential. This means explaining how AI systems arrive at their conclusions, making the underlying logic accessible to users and stakeholders. Transparency fosters trust, allowing individuals to understand and verify the actions and decisions made by AI systems. Engaging diverse stakeholders in the AI development process further enhances responsibility. Organizations can identify and address potential biases by involving individuals from various backgrounds and perspectives before they manifest in AI applications. This collaborative approach ensures that AI systems are designed inclusively, promoting fairness and equity.

The role of AI ethics committees is crucial in overseeing the responsible use of AI technologies. These committees provide the necessary oversight to ensure that AI initiatives adhere to ethical standards. By establishing ethics committees, organizations can create a structured environment where moral considerations are systematically addressed. These committees evaluate AI projects, identify potential ethical issues, and recommend solutions to mitigate risks. They serve as a check-and-balance system, holding developers and organizations accountable for the moral implications of their AI systems. Through regular assessments and evaluations, ethics committees play a vital role in maintaining the integrity and credibility of AI technologies.

Several organizations have already taken the lead in demonstrating responsible AI practices. Companies like IBM have implemented fairness audits in their AI systems, ensuring their technologies do not perpetuate biases or discrimination. These audits involve rigorous testing and evaluation of AI models to identify and rectify potential biases. By proactively addressing fairness, these companies set a benchmark for ethical AI development, showcasing the importance of accountability in technological innovation. Government initiatives also play a significant role in promoting ethical AI standards. For example, various governments have established regulatory frameworks that mandate ethical considerations in AI deployment. These initiatives create a legal and moral foundation that guides organizations in responsible AI use, fostering a culture of trust and accountability.

The pursuit of responsible AI use is a multifaceted endeavor that requires continuous effort and collaboration. It involves a commitment to ethical principles, transparency, and inclusivity, ensuring that AI technologies align with human values and societal needs. Organizations can build trust with their users and stakeholders by prioritizing responsible AI practices, demonstrating that technology can be a force for good. As AI continues evolving and permeating various aspects of life, responsible use becomes increasingly imperative. Through these best practices, we can navigate the complexities of AI, ensuring that its advancements benefit society as a whole.

Chapter 4 Self-Assessment

As you reflect on the ethical landscape of artificial intelligence, consider the multifaceted nature of AI ethics and its implications for both personal and professional spheres. At the heart of AI ethics lies the principle of fairness, which demands that AI systems operate without bias, treating all individuals equitably, irrespective of their demographic background. This principle is not merely a theoretical ideal but a practical necessity. It ensures that AI systems do not perpetuate existing societal inequalities. To evaluate fairness, consider how well you can identify potential biases in AI applications you encounter, whether in social media algorithms, recruitment processes, or customer service interactions. This awareness is critical, empowering you to advocate for technologies that promote equality and inclusivity.

Data privacy forms another cornerstone of AI ethics, underscoring the need to protect personal information in an increasingly digital world. As AI systems collect and analyze vast amounts of data, safeguarding privacy becomes paramount to preventing the misuse of sensitive information. Reflect on your understanding of data privacy principles and the measures you can take to protect your data. Consider how well you grasp the legal frameworks designed to uphold your privacy rights, such as GDPR and CCPA. These regulations are not just bureaucratic formalities but a commitment to respecting individual autonomy and fostering trust in the digital ecosystem. By recognizing the importance of data privacy, you contribute to a culture that values transparency and accountability.

AI's societal impact extends beyond individual sectors, shaping the broader contours of social interactions and global challenges. As AI systems influence everything from climate solutions to healthcare accessibility, they offer unprecedented opportunities to improve quality of life. However, these advancements come with ethical dilemmas that require careful consideration.

Reflect on your ability to engage with these ethical questions, balancing the promise of innovation with the need for responsible deployment. This involves understanding the potential consequences of AI on social dynamics, privacy, and governance. By critically assessing AI's societal impact, you contribute to a discourse that prioritizes ethical considerations and seeks to harness technology for the greater good. Consider your understanding of best practices for responsible AI, including transparency in algorithmic processes and the involvement of diverse stakeholders. By supporting the establishment of AI ethics committees and advocating for fairness audits, you promote accountability and trust in AI technologies. This commitment to ethical practices ensures that AI serves humanity's best interests, fostering a future where technology enhances rather than undermines societal values.

As you conclude this reflection, recognize the interconnectedness of AI ethics with broader societal issues. The principles of fairness, privacy, and responsibility are not isolated concepts but interwoven elements that shape the ethical framework of AI. By understanding and applying these principles, you contribute to a world where AI technologies are developed and used with integrity and foresight. This chapter has explored the ethical dimensions of AI, emphasizing the importance of vigilance and advocacy in navigating the complexities of AI ethics. As AI continues to evolve, the need for ethical stewardship grows, underscoring the imperative to engage with these issues thoughtfully and proactively.

FREE GOODWILL

Someone wise once said, "Money can't buy happiness."

Well, whoever said that hasn't given enough of it away! Think about it: people who give generously without expecting anything in return tend to live longer, feel happier, and—ironically—even make more money. Sounds pretty good, right?

Since we've got some time together, you bet I'm gonna take a swing at making that happen right here, right now. So, here's a quick question: Would you help someone you've never even met if it cost you absolutely nothing, and you didn't even get credit for it? Intrigued? Great, let me explain.

Who is this mysterious stranger you'd be helping? Well, they're a lot like you—or at least, they're where you once were. They're less experienced regarding AI and fired up to make a difference, but they may be feeling a little stuck and unsure where to turn. Ava Sinclair Publishing ´s mission is simple yet powerful: We want to empower readers with accessible, insightful content on technology and artificial intelligence. We want to simplify complex topics and equip readers to navigate today's evolving tech landscape confidently. Everything we do revolves around that goal, and reaching as many people as possible is the only way to get there.

That's where you come in.

The truth is, most people judge a book by its cover—and definitely by its reviews. So, here's my humble ask on behalf of an entrepreneur who's struggling right now, someone you've never met but who's doing their best to chase their dreams:

Could you spare a moment to help that entrepreneur by leaving a quick review for this book? Seriously, it'll cost you zero dollars and less than 60 seconds of your time—but your review might genuinely change someone's life forever. Your words could help one more person struggling with technology and artificial intelligence, provide or increase a paycheck for someone's family, give someone sustainable work, or even make a fellow entrepreneur's dream come true. That sounds pretty rewarding, doesn't it?

So, if you're ready to get that amazing feel-good buzz and help out in a big way, all you gotta do is take less than a minute right now to leave a review here:

Easy as pie.

If you're on Audible, just tap those three little dots in the top-right corner of your device, hit "Rate and Review," leave a quick sentence or two along with a star rating, and voilà—you just made someone's day!

Thank you for being someone who makes a difference.

Let's spread some goodwill together!

5

EXPLORING AI TECHNOLOGIES

Our reality is increasingly shaped by artificial intelligence. AI applications have seamlessly integrated into everyday life, influencing diverse fields and reshaping how we interact with technology. From personalized virtual assistants to creative digital tools, AI algorithms now play an essential role in enhancing precision, efficiency, and responsiveness across numerous applications. As AI continues to evolve, it transforms ordinary experiences into opportunities for greater productivity, creativity, and convenience.

Virtual assistants, for instance, have revolutionized routine tasks. Whether setting reminders, sending messages, or controlling smart home devices, these tools offer intuitive interactions by leveraging AI-powered natural language processing. Customizing settings to match your preferences, such as adjusting voice options or integrating additional apps, further enhances their practicality.

The transformative power of AI technologies extends well beyond personal convenience, influencing major industries through deep learning, automation, augmented reality (AR), the

Internet of Things (IoT), and sophisticated chatbot systems. This chapter explores AI's distinct yet interconnected aspects, highlighting their practical applications, benefits, challenges, and future developments. Understanding these facets of AI technology will provide a comprehensive view of how they collectively shape our digital and physical worlds, setting the stage for exploring their broader societal implications.

Exercise for You: Audit Your AI App Usage

Take a moment to review the AI applications you use regularly. Consider how they enhance your daily life and whether you leverage their full potential. Examine the permissions you have granted and adjust them if necessary to protect your privacy. This exercise encourages you to think critically about your interactions with AI, ensuring a balance between convenience and security.

5.1 DEEP LEARNING: GOING BEYOND BASICS

Deep learning is a significant advancement in artificial intelligence, characterized by its ability to process complex patterns and make predictions based on extensive data sets. Deep learning employs multilayer neural networks inspired by the human brain's structure and function. These networks consist of interconnected nodes, or neurons, organized into layers that process information progressively. Each layer captures different levels of abstraction, from basic features to more intricate patterns. This layered approach allows deep learning models to handle vast amounts of data, extracting meaningful insights that traditional methods might overlook. Unlike conventional machine learning, which often requires manual feature extraction, deep learning autonomously identifies relevant features, reducing human intervention. Graphics processing units (GPUs) are pivotal in deep learning, as they accelerate computations by handling multiple tasks simultaneously. This capability is crucial because deep learning models demand significant computational power to train effectively. GPUs enable these models to process large datasets quickly, facilitating the discovery of complex correlations within the data.

Key architectures in deep learning, such as Convolutional Neural Networks (CNNs), Recurrent Neural Networks (RNNs), and Transformer models, have revolutionized various fields. CNNs are particularly adept at image recognition, leveraging their ability to process spatial hierarchies in visual data. By utilizing filters to detect patterns like edges and textures, CNNs can accurately classify images. This technology underpins applications ranging from facial recognition systems to autonomous vehicles, where real-time image analysis is crucial. Meanwhile, RNNs excel in handling sequential data, making them ideal for tasks like speech recognition and language translation. Their architecture allows them to retain information from previous inputs, providing context for current processing tasks. This capability is vital in applications where understanding the data sequence is essential, such as natural language processing and time-series prediction. Transformer models have emerged as a groundbreaking architecture for natural language processing tasks. Unlike RNNs, Transformers process entire data sequences simultaneously, enabling them to capture long-range dependencies more effectively. This architecture forms the basis of advanced language models, such as those used in chatbots and translation services, where capturing the nuances of human language is paramount.

The practical applications of deep learning are diverse and transformative, spanning numerous industries. Deep learning facilitates navigation in autonomous vehicles by interpreting sensor data to detect obstacles, road signs, and other vehicles. This real-time analysis is crucial for ensuring safe and efficient autonomous driving. Healthcare also benefits significantly from deep learning, particularly in diagnostics. Deep learning models can analyze medical images, such as X-rays and MRIs, to identify abnormalities with precision comparable to human experts. This capability accelerates diagnosis, enabling timely treatment interventions. Additionally, deep learning is instrumental in drug discovery, predicting molecular interactions and potential drug efficacy, and streamlining new therapies' development.

However, deep learning's advancements are not without challenges. One of the primary hurdles is the requirement for large datasets to train models effectively. High-quality, diverse data is essential for capturing the complexity of real-world scenarios. Without sufficient data, models risk overfitting, performing well on training data but failing to generalize to new inputs. Regularization techniques, such as dropout and weight decay, mitigate this risk by preventing models from becoming too attuned to training data noise. Another significant challenge is the substantial computational power to train deep learning models. Training deep networks involves processing millions of parameters, which demands considerable resources and time. Despite these challenges, the potential of deep learning to drive innovation and solve complex problems continues to fuel research and development in this dynamic field.

5.2 AUTOMATION AND AI: STREAMLINING TASKS

In the modern world, automation has become synonymous with efficiency and innovation. When we talk about automation in the context of artificial intelligence, we refer to a sophisticated enhancement that makes processes not just automatic but also intelligent and adaptive. AI-powered systems can adjust to varying conditions and optimize performance without human intervention, making them invaluable across numerous sectors. Consider robotic process automation in business operations, where AI algorithms streamline repetitive tasks such as data entry and customer service inquiries. This automated efficiency allows human workers to focus on more strategic and creative tasks, enhancing overall productivity.

The advantages of implementing AI-driven automation are numerous and transformative. One of the most significant benefits is the increase in efficiency. Automated systems perform tasks faster than their human counterparts, reducing the time needed to complete processes. This speed reduces operational costs, as businesses can achieve more with fewer resources. Additionally, AI enhances accuracy and minimizes human error. This reliability can improve outcomes and reduce risks in industries where precision is crucial, such as finance and healthcare. By reducing errors, AI-driven automation enhances consistency, ensuring that tasks are always performed to the same high standard.

Automation's impact is evident across various industries, each benefiting from AI's transformative power. Automated assembly lines have revolutionized production by increasing output while ensuring consistent quality. Robots equipped with AI can work tirelessly, performing tasks with precision and speed that surpass human capabilities. The finance industry also reaps the benefits of automation through automated report generation. AI systems analyze financial data and produce comprehensive reports with accuracy and speed that humans struggle to match. In customer service, automated ticket triaging helps streamline the process of handling customer inquiries efficiently. AI systems categorize and prioritize tickets, allowing human agents to focus on more complex issues and improving response times and customer satisfaction.

The landscape of AI and automation is poised for even more exciting developments. The rise of intelligent virtual assistants is revolutionizing how we interact with technology in personal and professional contexts. These assistants will be capable of understanding and predicting user needs, providing proactive support that enhances productivity and convenience. Another significant trend is the emergence of fully autonomous factories and workplaces. AI systems will oversee operations in these environments, making real-time adjustments to optimize efficiency and resource use. This shift will redefine the nature of work, with humans taking on roles that require creativity, strategic thinking, and emotional intelligence. As automation continues to evolve, its potential to reshape industries and improve lives is limitless, promising a future where efficiency and innovation go hand in hand.

5.3 CHATBOTS: ENHANCING CUSTOMER EXPERIENCE

Entering an online store today often means encountering a friendly virtual assistant prepared to answer your questions around the clock. Chatbots have transformed customer service by providing continuous support 24/7 and instantaneous responses, efficiently addressing inquiries in ways human operators may struggle to match consistently. At the heart of chatbot functionality lies Natural Language Processing (NLP), empowering these digital assistants to understand the context and nuances of human language, resulting in natural, intuitive interactions. Additionally, as chatbots engage in more conversations, machine learning algorithms refine their capabilities, enhancing accuracy, relevance, and personalization with each interaction, ultimately delivering an increasingly tailored customer experience.

In e-commerce, chatbots have become indispensable tools for handling product inquiries and guiding users through buying. They can suggest products based on browsing history, answer questions about features, and even facilitate the checkout process—all within a single conversation. This integration streamlines the customer journey, reducing friction and enhancing satisfaction. Virtual assistants serve as an initial point of contact in healthcare, offering advice on symptoms and directing patients to appropriate resources. This accessibility ensures that individuals receive timely guidance, alleviating the burden on healthcare professionals. Meanwhile, in the banking sector, chatbots assist customers with account management, providing information on transactions and balances, and even facilitating money transfers. By automating these routine interactions, banks can allocate human resources to more complex tasks, improving overall service efficiency.

Despite their advantages, chatbots face challenges that can hinder their effectiveness. One significant obstacle is understanding complex or ambiguous queries. While chatbots excel at handling straightforward questions, they may struggle with idiomatic expressions or customers who convey frustration through sarcasm, complicating the task of accurately interpreting the message. They also struggle with queries requiring deeper contextual understanding or involving multiple information layers. Users might express themselves in colloquial terms or use language that the chatbot's algorithms have not encountered, leading to misunderstandings. The chatbot must understand the literal meaning of the words and the underlying sentiment and context to provide appropriate assistance. Maintaining a natural conversational flow is another challenge. Users expect interactions to mimic human conversations, with proper pacing and logical transitions. Achieving this level of sophistication requires ongoing refinement of the chatbot's NLP capabilities and dialogue management systems.

Addressing these limitations involves continuous improvement and optimization. Developers must regularly update and train chatbots to recognize and respond to emerging language patterns and user expectations. Additionally, implementing fallback mechanisms—such as transferring conversations to human agents when the chatbot reaches its limitations—can enhance user satisfaction. This dynamic integration between human and automated support ensures that customer interactions remain seamless and practical. As chatbots evolve, their role in improving customer experience will likely expand, offering even more sophisticated solutions tailored to each industry's unique needs.

Exercise for You: Evaluate Your Chatbot Interaction

Reflect on your recent experiences with chatbots, whether in online shopping, banking, or other services. Consider how these interactions influenced your experience. Did the chatbot meet your expectations in terms of responsiveness and understanding? Were there instances where you preferred human interaction? This reflection can help you recognize the strengths and limitations of chatbots in customer service and how they might evolve to better meet user needs.

5.4 AUGMENTED REALITY AND AI: BLENDING REALITIES

Augmented Reality (AR) represents a significant leap in how we perceive and interact with the digital world, offering a seamless blend of virtual elements with our physical surroundings. At the heart of this technology lies its integration with artificial intelligence, which enhances AR experiences by enabling real-time object detection and contextual understanding. Imagine wearing AR glasses that instantly overlay digital information onto the physical world—AI processes and identifies objects in your environment, providing relevant data and insights. This dynamic interaction between AI and AR enriches the visual experience and transforms how information is accessed and utilized in real-time. The interplay between these technologies is evident in various applications, where AI algorithms enhance the precision and responsiveness of AR systems, ensuring that the digital augmentation aligns seamlessly with the physical world.

In education, AR and AI combine to create immersive learning experiences that engage students in ways traditional methods cannot. Picture a classroom where historical events come to life through interactive AR displays, allowing students to explore ancient civilizations or scientific phenomena firsthand. AI enhances these experiences by personalizing content based on individual learning needs, adapting to each student's pace and style. Similarly, AR and AI work together in retail to revolutionize the shopping experience. Virtual try-ons, powered by AI, allow customers to see how clothes or makeup look without physically trying them on. This enhances convenience and reduces return rates by helping consumers make more informed decisions. Product visualizations, enabled by AI-driven AR, provide detailed insights into product features and specifications, offering a richer and more engaging shopping experience.

The technological components that facilitate AR and AI collaboration are intricate and fascinating. Computer vision, a critical element, allows AR systems to map the environment accurately, interpreting spatial data to overlay virtual objects precisely. This technology ensures that digital elements appear as natural extensions of the physical world, maintaining alignment even as the user moves. AI algorithms further refine these interactions by analyzing data from sensors and cameras, allowing AR systems to adapt dynamically to environmental changes. This adaptability ensures a fluid and cohesive experience, where digital content responds intelligently to user actions and environmental conditions, creating a more realistic and satisfying interaction.

Looking to the future, the potential for innovations in AR and AI is vast, with numerous possibilities on the horizon. One exciting development is AI-enhanced AR for remote collaboration, where teams across the globe can interact with shared digital environments as if they were in the same room. This could revolutionize fields like design and engineering, allowing real-time collaboration on complex projects. Advancements in wearable AR devices are also anticipated, promising more comfortable and versatile technology that integrates seamlessly into daily life. Imagine glasses that provide real-time language translation or navigation assistance, adapting to your needs without interrupting your flow. These innovations promise to redefine how we interact with digital content, making technology an even more integral part of our everyday lives.

5.5 INTERNET OF THINGS: CONNECTING THE WORLD

The Internet of Things (IoT) is a transformative technology that connects everyday objects to the internet, enabling them to send, receive, and act upon data. At the heart of IoT's innovation is its relationship with artificial intelligence, which imbues these connected devices with intelligence and autonomy. AI-driven analytics play a crucial role in processing the vast amounts of data generated by IoT devices, extracting valuable insights that inform decision-making and enhance functionality. Imagine a network of devices in a smart home, from thermostats to security cameras, communicating seamlessly to optimize energy use and security. AI analyzes usage patterns and external conditions, making real-time adjustments that improve efficiency and comfort without human intervention.

Integrating AI with IoT offers numerous benefits, enhancing operational efficiency and user experience. One of the most significant advantages is predictive maintenance, which relies on AI to analyze data from sensors embedded in machinery. Predictive maintenance minimizes downtime and extends equipment lifespan by identifying potential failures before they occur. This proactive approach is particularly valuable in industries where equipment reliability is critical, such as manufacturing and transportation. AI-enhanced IoT also personalizes user experiences, offering services tailored to individual preferences and behaviors. For instance, a smart home system might adjust lighting and temperature based on the homeowner's habits, creating a comfortable and intuitive environment.

How AI and IoT are interplaying well is evident across various sectors, each benefiting from the enhanced capabilities of these technologies. Precision farming utilizes IoT sensors to monitor soil conditions, weather patterns, and crop health in agriculture. AI processes this data to optimize irrigation, fertilization, and pest control, maximizing yield while minimizing resource use. Smart cities leverage IoT and AI to manage urban infrastructure efficiently, optimizing traffic flow and resource allocation. Sensors embedded in roads and public transport systems provide real-time data that AI algorithms use to predict congestion and adjust traffic signals accordingly. These applications demonstrate the potential of AI and IoT to improve quality of life, enhance sustainability, and drive economic growth.

Despite their promise, integrating AI and IoT presents challenges that must be addressed to ensure successful implementation. Data security and privacy are significant concerns, as the proliferation of connected devices increases the risk of unauthorized access and data breaches. Protecting sensitive information requires robust encryption protocols and security measures that safeguard data in transit and at rest. Additionally, the interoperability of diverse IoT devices poses a challenge, as varying standards and protocols can hinder communication and integration. Ensuring compatibility among devices from different manufacturers is essential for creating cohesive and efficient IoT ecosystems. Addressing these challenges requires collaboration among stakeholders, including developers, manufacturers, and regulatory bodies, to establish standards and practices that support secure, interoperable IoT solutions.

Chapter 5 Self-Assessment

Reflecting on the vast landscape of AI technologies explored in this chapter offers a unique opportunity to evaluate your understanding and application of these groundbreaking innovations. Considering the myriad ways AI has integrated into various aspects of life and industry, it's crucial to assess how well you comprehend and can utilize these concepts. Begin by revisiting the core ideas presented, from the transformative power of AI in streamlining tasks to its role in enhancing customer interactions. Consider how automation's efficiency and precision have reshaped industries, enabling the quick and accurate completion of tasks. This reflection is not just about recalling facts but understanding the practical implications of these technologies.

Think about how chatbots revolutionize customer service by providing consistent and immediate responses, drawing on sophisticated algorithms to interpret and respond to inquiries. Their integration into sectors like e-commerce and healthcare showcases AI's capacity to improve user experiences while alleviating human workload. Assess your understanding of how chatbots balance advanced technology with the need for natural, human-like conversations. Equally important is your understanding of augmented reality's blending of digital and physical realms. Reflect on how AI enhances these experiences, creating immersive environments for education and retail. Consider the technological components, such as computer vision, that enable these advancements and the future innovations that will continue to redefine interaction with digital content. The Internet of Things represents another dimension of AI's potential, connecting devices to create more innovative environments.

Assess your understanding of how AI-driven analytics optimize operations and enhance user experiences across domains, from agriculture to urban planning, as you ponder all these connections. Recognize the challenges accompanying these innovations, like data security, and consider how interoperability between devices can be achieved. This reflection should also involve a self-assessment of your ability to identify knowledge gaps. Search for specific AI quizzes on the internet and test yourself. This active engagement with the material ensures that your learning is dynamic and evolving, adapting to the ever-changing landscape of AI technology.

By actively engaging with the material, you deepen your understanding and can apply these insights to real-world scenarios. This approach reinforces your knowledge and empowers you to stay ahead in a rapidly evolving technological landscape. As you conclude this chapter, consider how these technologies interconnect to form a comprehensive understanding of AI's role in modern life. This reflection positions you to explore AI's ethical implications and societal impacts, which will be the focus of the next chapter.

6

AI TOOLS AND RESOURCES FOR CONTINUED LEARNING

Imagine waking up on a Saturday morning with a fresh cup of coffee; just last night, you finished reading this book, and now you feel ready to dive into AI without leaving the comfort of your home. With the rise of online learning platforms, exploring artificial intelligence has never been easier or more accessible. This chapter serves as your practical guide, introducing you to diverse resources and tools tailored to different learning styles, goals, and schedules, all designed to make mastering AI accessible and enjoyable.

In the following sections, you'll discover various resources, from interactive online courses to vibrant peer communities and comprehensive reading materials. Whether you want to deepen your understanding through insightful articles, engage actively in AI workshops, or connect with others who share your enthusiasm, these resources will empower you on your journey toward AI proficiency. Embrace the wealth of knowledge awaiting you, and begin exploring the many paths that lead to confident, informed participation in an AI-driven world.

6.1 EMBRACING ONLINE LEARNING: YOUR GATEWAY TO AI MASTERY

Online courses have revolutionized education, allowing you to explore complex subjects like artificial intelligence at your own pace and schedule. Whether you're a curious beginner or looking to advance your skills, there are platforms tailored to meet your learning needs, offering a range of courses from introductory to advanced levels.

Coursera stands out as a leader among these platforms, providing courses from renowned universities such as Stanford and institutions like Google. A wealth of courses offer comprehensive insights into AI, covering fundamental concepts and advanced applications. I do not want to give any specific course recommendations here - as the level and pace of courses are too individual. But Coursera's partnership with top-tier educational entities ensures that you receive rigorous and relevant education, equipping you with the knowledge to navigate the AI landscape confidently. Similarly, edX offers access to university-level courses across various subjects, including AI, making it an excellent choice for those seeking a broad array of learning opportunities.

Selecting the right course is crucial to your success and satisfaction. Begin by assessing your current knowledge and understanding of AI (check out the Interactive Exercise below). Choosing courses that match your skill level is essential, ensuring you are neither overwhelmed nor under-challenged. Please pay attention to course prerequisites, as they offer clues about the complexity of the material. Reading course reviews and ratings can also provide valuable insights into the course quality and past learners' experiences. By taking these steps, you ensure that your chosen course aligns with your learning goals and sets you on a path to success. Additionally, online learning connects you with a global community of learners and instructors, fostering collaboration and knowledge sharing. Engaging in discussions with diverse perspectives enriches your learning experience and provides a deeper understanding of AI's multifaceted nature.

Exercise for You: Creating Your Learning Plan

Take a moment to outline your learning plan for AI. Consider your current knowledge level, learning goals, and the time you can dedicate each week. Identify potential courses on platforms like Coursera or edX that align with your objectives. Set specific milestones for completing modules or projects and establish a regular study schedule. This exercise will help you organize your learning journey and remain focused and motivated.

As you embark on this educational path for learning about AI, remember that online learning is about acquiring knowledge and fostering a mindset of curiosity and continuous exploration. The digital age offers unprecedented access to resources and information, empowering you to learn and grow at your own pace. Embrace this opportunity to deepen your understanding of AI and take advantage of the many courses and platforms available. By doing so, you equip yourself with the tools needed to thrive in an increasingly AI-driven world.

6.2 AI SOFTWARE AND KITS: PRACTICAL TOOLS FOR BEGINNERS

Exploring the world of AI can be daunting, but with the right tools, it becomes an engaging and rewarding experience. Beginner-friendly AI software and kits provide a hands-on approach to learning, turning complex theories into tangible projects. These tools demystify AI concepts by allowing you to experiment with real-world applications in a user-friendly environment. For instance, TensorFlow Playground is an excellent entry point for those interested in neural networks. This visual tool lets you manipulate parameters and see how changes affect outcomes, making it easier to grasp the intricacies of neural networks. By interacting with the tool, you can experiment with different scenarios and build an intuitive understanding of how neural networks process information. Another powerful resource is IBM Watson Studio, which offers a collaborative environment for data scientists. This platform combines machine learning with data analysis, providing the infrastructure for project collaboration. Its versatile nature supports various data science activities, from data preparation to model deployment.

Getting started with AI software may seem challenging, but you can easily set up these tools with the proper guidance. Installation guides are crucial for ensuring that your software functions smoothly. Many AI frameworks offer detailed instructions to help you download and configure the necessary components. These guides typically include information on system requirements and step-by-step processes to ensure you're fully equipped to begin your exploration. Additionally, community forums and documentation can be invaluable resources when encountering challenges. Engaging with these resources facilitates the setup process and connects you with a network of learners and experts willing to share insights and solutions. By following these steps, you can overcome any initial hurdles and focus on the exciting task of experimentation and learning.

Once your tools are set up, it's time to delve into their features and capabilities. Many AI software platforms offer drag-and-drop interfaces, simplifying the process of building models. These interfaces allow you to construct complex systems without extensive code, making AI more accessible to those without a technical background. Furthermore, integration with cloud services provides scalable computing power, enabling you to work with large datasets and sophisticated models. This feature is particularly beneficial for projects that require significant processing capabilities, allowing you to explore AI's potential without being limited by hardware constraints. By leveraging these functionalities, you can tackle ambitious projects and better understand AI's transformative power.

Encouraging exploration and experimentation is key to mastering AI tools. As you become more comfortable with the software, consider creating small projects to test different AI concepts. This hands-on approach reinforces theoretical knowledge and builds practical skills. Start with simple projects, such as developing a basic image recognition model, and gradually increase complexity as your confidence grows. Many platforms offer built-in tutorials and examples to guide your learning journey. These resources provide valuable insights into best practices and common pitfalls, helping you navigate challenges and refine your approach. By actively engaging with the software, you enhance your technical skills and foster a mindset of curiosity and innovation.

6.3 TECH BLOGS AND PODCASTS: STAYING INFORMED

In the ever-evolving landscape of artificial intelligence, staying informed is beneficial and necessary. With the rapid pace of advancements and innovations, keeping up with the latest developments can feel like an uphill battle. This is where reputable tech blogs and websites become invaluable resources. One such resource is Towards Data Science, a publication on Medium that delves into a wide array of AI topics. It offers insights from industry experts, practical guides, and thought-provoking analyses. Whether you're interested in the technical intricacies of machine learning algorithms or the broader implications of AI in society, this platform provides content that caters to diverse interests and expertise levels.

Another noteworthy source is AI Trends, which focuses on the intersection of business and technology within the AI realm. It provides updates on cutting-edge AI applications and explores how they are reshaping industries. This blog is handy for those interested in understanding AI's impact on business strategies and market dynamics. By regularly engaging with such content, you stay informed and gain a deeper appreciation for the multifaceted nature of AI and its potential to drive transformative change.

Equally enriching are AI podcasts, which offer a unique auditory experience for learning and reflection. The AI Alignment Podcast, for example, explores AI's technical and philosophical dimensions. Through in-depth discussions and interviews with leading experts, the podcast examines how AI can be aligned with human values and ethical standards. Listening to these conversations can broaden your perspective and provide insights into the complex challenges and opportunities AI presents. Podcasts such as these offer an engaging way to deepen your understanding, especially during activities like commuting or exercising, making efficient use of time that might otherwise be idle.

Diverse content consumption is crucial for a well-rounded understanding of AI. Technical articles provide the rigor and detail necessary to grasp complex concepts, while opinion pieces offer subjective interpretations that challenge your thinking. By blending these perspectives, you cultivate a more holistic view of AI. This approach allows you to appreciate not just the technical feats of AI but also its societal implications and ethical considerations. Engaging with various content types encourages critical thinking and helps you form well-informed opinions.

To effectively integrate tech blogs and podcasts into your routine, consider setting up systems that facilitate regular consumption. One practical strategy is subscribing to RSS feeds for your favorite blogs, ensuring you're notified of new content without checking multiple sites manually. This setup streamlines your information intake, allowing you to focus on reading and reflecting. Similarly, incorporating podcasts into your daily activities can make learning seamless. Whether driving, walking, or doing household chores, podcasts can provide a steady stream of information and inspiration. By intentionally weaving these resources into your day-to-day life, you maximize your exposure to valuable insights and stay attuned to the dynamic world of AI.

🧩 **Exercise for You: Your AI Information Diet**

Take a moment to assess the tech blogs and podcasts you currently consume. Consider how these sources contribute to your understanding of AI and identify gaps in your information diet. Are there perspectives or topics you feel are underrepresented? Create a plan to diversify your content sources, ensuring a balanced and comprehensive view of the AI landscape. This exercise encourages ongoing reflection and adaptation, helping you remain informed and engaged in AI.

By consistently engaging with reliable blogs and thought-provoking podcasts, you position yourself to stay at the forefront of AI developments. These resources inform and inspire, equipping you with the knowledge and insight needed to navigate the complexities of AI with confidence.

6.4 BOOKS AND ARTICLES: DEEPENING YOUR UNDERSTANDING

Immersing yourself in AI through books and articles can profoundly enrich your understanding. After reading this book as a beginner, you continue to read with more advanced AI knowledge. There are plenty of books to deepen your understanding of AI and its real-world applications. While online courses provide structured learning, books dive deeper into AI principles, histories, and methodologies. For those seeking a comprehensive overview of AI, "Artificial Intelligence: A Guide to Intelligent Systems" by Michael Negnevitsky is an excellent starting point. This book simplifies complex ideas and introduces you to intelligent systems with clarity, making it accessible for those new to the field. By engaging with foundational texts, you gain a solid grounding and context for the more advanced concepts you may encounter later.

For those ready to tackle the intricacies of AI, "Deep Learning" by Ian Goodfellow, Yoshua Bengio, and Aaron Courville stands as a seminal work. This book delves into the depths of deep learning, offering insights into neural networks and their capabilities. It thoroughly explores the mathematics and theories underpinning these systems, equipping you with the knowledge to understand and apply advanced AI techniques. By investing time in such comprehensive works, you gain a deeper appreciation for AI's complexities and enhance your ability to engage with technical discussions and innovations.

Expanding your understanding of AI also involves exploring articles that offer advanced insights into specific topics. Research papers and case studies provide an avenue for in-depth exploration of AI applications and advancements. These articles often present cutting-edge research and innovative solutions, allowing you to stay abreast of the latest developments in the field. Engaging with these materials sharpens your analytical skills and enriches your perspective with diverse viewpoints. Articles serve as a bridge between foundational knowledge and current trends, ensuring that your understanding of AI remains both comprehensive and contemporary.

Implement strategies that enhance understanding and retention to maximize the benefits of reading. Taking notes is a powerful tool for capturing key points and reflections, allowing you to revisit and reinforce your learning. Summarizing chapters or articles helps distill complex ideas into digestible insights, making it easier to recall information later. Discussing readings with peers can deepen your understanding, as conversations often reveal different interpretations and applications. Discussions cultivate a collaborative learning environment where ideas are exchanged, refined, and expanded upon. This collaborative approach enhances your ability to articulate concepts clearly and apply them practically.

Exercise for You: Reading Reflection Checklist

Consider creating a reading reflection checklist to aid in your exploration of AI literature and advance your reading notes. This checklist can include prompts such as identifying key themes, noting any questions that arise, and summarizing insights gained. Use this tool to guide your reading sessions, ensuring you engage actively with the material. Reflecting on your readings fosters a deeper connection to the content and enhances comprehension and retention.

6.5 AI WORKSHOPS AND EVENTS: LEARNING LIVE

As you step into a bustling conference hall filled with innovators, technologists, and thought leaders eager to share insights on artificial intelligence, you experience the dynamic atmosphere characteristic of AI conferences and workshops. Such events are vibrant hubs where diverse ideas and expertise converge, sparking innovation and new possibilities. Attending these gatherings offers an exceptional opportunity to immerse yourself in the latest developments in AI. Notably, the AI Summit Series is one influential event that highlights industry-specific applications, bringing together professionals from multiple sectors to exchange knowledge and showcase practical implementations. Likewise, NeurIPS, a premier machine learning and computational neuroscience conference, attracts global researchers and practitioners and is renowned for its presentations on groundbreaking research and specialized workshops. These events deepen your understanding of AI and connect you with a community of passionate, like-minded individuals.

The benefits of attending live AI events extend far beyond the acquisition of knowledge. These gatherings offer invaluable networking opportunities, enabling you to interact with industry leaders, researchers, and potential collaborators. Engaging in conversations with experts allows you to gain insights into the latest trends and challenges facing the AI landscape. Additionally, exposure to cutting-edge research and technologies provides a glimpse into the future of AI, equipping you with the foresight needed to anticipate and adapt to forthcoming developments. This firsthand experience with emerging innovations can inspire new ideas and approaches, fostering a spirit of creativity and curiosity. Moreover, workshops and breakout sessions provide hands-on learning experiences, allowing you to apply theoretical knowledge to practical scenarios. These interactive sessions often involve collaborative problem-solving exercises, enhancing your ability to work effectively in team settings. By actively participating in these activities, you reinforce your understanding of AI concepts and develop essential skills highly valued in the industry.

Preparation is key to maximizing the value of attending live events. Before the conference begins, take the time to research the agenda and identify sessions that align with your interests and goals. Preparing questions and topics for discussion can help you engage more meaningfully with speakers and fellow attendees. This proactive approach ensures you make the most of your interactions and derive maximum benefit from the event. During the conference, remain open to new experiences and ideas and seize opportunities to participate in workshops and breakout sessions. These smaller, focused gatherings often provide deeper insights and more personalized learning experiences. Engaging actively with presenters and peers can lead to fruitful exchanges of knowledge and perspectives, enriching your overall experience. Finally, take advantage of networking events and social gatherings to build lasting connections. These informal settings offer a relaxed environment for discussing shared interests and exploring potential collaborations.

6.6 AI COMMUNITIES AND FORUMS: CONNECTING WITH PEERS

In the vast and dynamic field of artificial intelligence, individual learning can be significantly enriched by connecting with others with similar interests and challenges. Engaging with AI communities and forums provides a platform for sharing knowledge, seeking advice, and staying updated on the latest trends. One of the most prominent communities is Kaggle, a sprawling platform hosting data science competitions and a collaborative space for enthusiasts and professionals alike. Kaggle allows you to participate in various challenges, offering a hands-on approach to solving real-world problems and honing your AI skills. It provides access to many datasets and notebooks, enabling you to practice and experiment with different techniques. Beyond competitions, Kaggle fosters a supportive environment where you can connect with over 22 million members, exchange ideas, and learn from others' experiences. Reddit's r/MachineLearning is another valuable resource, functioning as a lively forum dedicated to discussions about AI. This subreddit offers a space to engage in conversations about recent research, ask questions, and share insights with a diverse community of AI enthusiasts. These platforms exemplify the open and collaborative nature of the AI field, where sharing knowledge and experiences contributes to collective growth.

Engaging with these communities or local AI meetups offers numerous benefits beyond simple knowledge acquisition. Local AI meetups are smaller gatherings, which can be a great way to stay engaged with the local AI community. Local meetups provide a platform for sharing experiences, discussing challenges, and exploring new ideas in a more intimate setting. By participating in local events, you can build a network of peers who share your passion for AI and are eager to collaborate on projects and initiatives. These connections can lead to valuable mentorship, support, and collaboration opportunities, enhancing your learning journey and professional growth. Engaging with local meetups also informs you about regional developments and opportunities in AI, ensuring you remain connected to the broader AI ecosystem.

Opportunities for collaboration abound within these communities, allowing you to work with peers on projects and challenges. Engaging in collaborative projects enhances your practical skills and exposes you to diverse perspectives and approaches. These experiences can deepen your understanding of AI and inspire creative solutions to complex problems. Participating in community challenges and hackathons is another avenue for collaboration. These events often simulate real-world scenarios, providing a platform to apply your knowledge and creativity in a competitive yet supportive setting. Hackathons, in particular, encourage rapid prototyping and innovation, pushing you to think critically and work efficiently under time constraints. Through these collaborative efforts, you can build a portfolio of projects that showcase your abilities and demonstrate your commitment to continuous learning.

Exercise for You: Building Your Network

Reflect on your current involvement with AI communities and forums. Are there platforms you frequently engage with, or are there new communities you wish to explore? Consider how participation in these spaces can enhance your learning and professional development. Identify specific goals for joining these communities, such as seeking mentorship, collaborating on projects, or staying informed about industry trends. This reflection can guide your efforts to build a network of supportive peers and mentors, enriching your AI journey.

Chapter 6 Self-Assessment

Reflecting on your journey through the diverse realms of AI learning resources is an invaluable exercise that can reveal much about your progress and future direction. As you assess your engagement with these tools, consider the breadth and depth of resources you've explored. Have you ventured into online courses that provide structured learning or experimented with AI software that offers a hands-on approach to understanding complex algorithms? Each resource type plays a unique role in expanding your AI knowledge, offering different perspectives and insights that contribute to a well-rounded understanding of the subject.

Think about the strategies you employed when selecting AI resources. Did you prioritize specific platforms for their reputation or the depth of their content? Consider how effectively these choices have aligned with your learning goals. Selecting the right resources is akin to choosing the best path on a map; it guides you to your destination efficiently and purposefully. Reflect on the skills you have developed or enhanced through these resources. Whether it's coding proficiency, analytical thinking, or problem-solving, each skill contributes to your overall competency in AI. Identifying gaps or areas for improvement is a vital part of this self-assessment, encouraging you to seek out additional resources or change your approach to meet your objectives better.

Engaging with expert content is another critical aspect of your learning journey. Whether through tech blogs, podcasts, or community forums, interacting with experts' insights can significantly enrich your understanding. Reflect on how these interactions have influenced your perspective on AI. Has engaging with expert content opened new avenues of thought or challenged existing beliefs? Consider the value of diverse content in providing a comprehensive view of AI's potential and challenges. Engaging with experts enhances your knowledge and connects you to a broader community of learners and professionals. This network can offer support, guidance, and inspiration as you continue to explore AI's evolving landscape. Moreover, the practical application of your acquired knowledge is where theory meets reality. Whether through collaborative projects, participation in hackathons, or personal experimentation, applying what you've learned solidifies concepts and enhances retention.

Reflect on the practical skills you've developed and how they have been implemented in real-world contexts. Consider these experiences' impact on your confidence and ability to tackle complex AI challenges. Practical application transforms abstract concepts into tangible skills, enabling you to contribute meaningfully to projects and discussions within the AI community. As you assess your progress, consider setting new goals to guide your ongoing exploration of AI. These goals may involve delving deeper into specific AI technologies, expanding your network, or exploring ethical considerations in AI development. By setting clear objectives, you maintain focus and motivation, ensuring continued growth and advancement in your understanding of AI. Remember, the field of AI is dynamic and ever-changing, offering endless opportunities for learning and discovery. Embrace these opportunities with curiosity and enthusiasm, knowing that your efforts contribute to a greater understanding of AI's role in shaping the future.

In summary, this self-assessment acts as a compass guiding you through your AI learning journey. By thoughtfully examining your experiences, strategies, and achievements, you uncover valuable insights into your growth and identify areas ripe for further development and learning. Embracing reflection nurtures a proactive mindset, empowering you to confidently navigate AI's complexities with clarity and intention. As you transition into the final chapter, keep open to new experiences, challenges, and continuous learning opportunities. Your dedication to ongoing improvement and innovative thinking will pave the way for a deeper understanding and appreciation of AI's transformative power.

7

EMPOWERMENT AND FUTURE EXPLORATION IN AI

AI reshapes our daily lives by enhancing productivity, convenience, and well-being. Smart home technologies, such as thermostats automatically adjusting to your schedule, improve comfort while conserving energy. Similarly, AI-driven fitness and health apps deliver personalized insights, tracking your activities, suggesting tailored workouts, and providing dietary advice customized to your health objectives.

Embracing AI with an open and positive mindset is crucial to unlocking its potential fully. When viewed as a supportive collaborator rather than a competitor, AI can amplify your abilities, complementing your strengths and filling gaps in your skills. This outlook encourages exploration, innovation, and flexibility, empowering you to adapt confidently to and benefit from the ongoing advancements in AI.

7.1 LIFELONG AI LEARNING: STAYING AHEAD OF AI TRENDS AND STAYING CURIOUS

Fostering a lifelong learning mindset is essential in a rapidly evolving technological landscape, particularly in the field of artificial intelligence. AI's rapid advancements and transformative power demand continuous engagement and an adaptable approach to learning. Cultivating curiosity and openness toward new technological developments keeps you aligned with the latest innovations, helping you navigate an environment where AI consistently reshapes industries and redefines traditional roles.

Establishing clear, actionable strategies is crucial to sustain effective lifelong learning. Setting specific, measurable learning goals aligned with your interests and professional aspirations provides a solid foundation. For example, you might plan to master a new programming language or explore an emerging AI application within a designated timeframe. Regularly evaluating your progress against these goals ensures consistent development and allows you to adjust your learning path as necessary. Additionally, diversifying your educational sources—such as books, online courses, workshops, and real-world experiences —provides a comprehensive understanding of AI. Each resource type contributes unique insights, enhancing your overall knowledge and flexibility.

Beyond expanding your expertise, lifelong learning significantly contributes to personal and professional growth by enhancing adaptability, a critical skill in an AI-driven world. Quickly absorbing and applying new concepts allows you to respond effectively to technological advancements, maintaining relevance in your field. Moreover, engaging with diverse educational materials sharpens critical thinking and problem-solving skills, encouraging innovative solutions and informed decision-making—abilities highly valued in contemporary workplaces.

Staying informed about AI involves more than merely understanding its technologies; it requires an ongoing commitment to continuous education and adaptation. Regularly consulting industry reports and professional publications can help you remain current with AI trends, offering insights into new technologies, market changes, and potential applications across various sectors. Integrating these resources into your learning routine broadens your understanding of AI's evolving societal role, preparing you to anticipate changes and capitalize on emerging opportunities.

Curiosity remains one of your most valuable assets in staying ahead of AI developments. Delving deeper into the implications of AI through speculative fiction and futurist writings can stimulate imagination and foster innovative thinking. These explorations challenge conventional ideas and encourage you to consider novel approaches to problem-solving. By nurturing your curiosity, you remain open to new possibilities and actively engage in meaningful discussions about AI's societal impact.

Pursuing knowledge and consistently engaging with AI developments empowers you to thrive amid rapid technological change. Lifelong learning enhances your capabilities, positions you as an informed participant in the AI revolution, and equips you to navigate its complexities confidently. Remember, learning is an ongoing journey—one that continuously evolves alongside you, offering fresh opportunities for growth and discovery.

In summary, staying ahead of AI trends requires a balanced combination of knowledge, curiosity, and consistent engagement. By maintaining a proactive approach to learning, you position yourself to fully leverage AI's potential and adapt effectively to future innovations. Embracing curiosity and actively participating in conversations about AI's future ensures your continued relevance and effectiveness in a world profoundly shaped by technology.

Chapter 7 Self-Assessment

As you reach the end of the final chapter, it is an opportune moment to pause and reflect on the insights you have gathered about artificial intelligence and its role in your personal and professional life.

Evaluate your readiness to leverage AI for career growth and personal empowerment effectively. Begin by considering the skills you have identified as crucial for thriving in AI-related fields. Reflect on the technical proficiencies you have developed and assess your understanding of the ethical considerations surrounding AI's integration into various sectors. These elements are foundational to adapting to the ever-evolving demands of the AI landscape.

Next, consider your networking strategies to connect with the AI community. Have you actively sought opportunities to engage with industry professionals through conferences, webinars, or online forums? Evaluate the strength of your professional network and the extent to which you have built relationships that can provide mentorship, collaboration, and insight into emerging trends. Networking is not merely about expanding your contact list; it is about fostering meaningful connections to support your growth and enhance your understanding of AI's potential impact on your field.

Reflect on your commitment to lifelong learning and adaptability. Have you established a routine incorporating regular study and new technology exploration? Consider how you have diversified your learning methods to include a combination of formal education, practical experience, and informal exploration. Lifelong learning is a continuous process that requires both discipline and curiosity. It involves setting goals, seeking feedback, and adapting your strategies as you encounter new challenges and opportunities. Assess how well you have integrated these practices into your daily life and how they have contributed to your personal and professional development.

Finally, as you reflect on these areas, consider how they collectively contribute to your readiness to embrace AI's potential. The insights gained from this self-assessment will help you identify areas for further growth and development. Use this opportunity to set new goals, reinforce your strengths, and address gaps in your knowledge or skills. Remember that the journey of learning and adaptation is ongoing, and your commitment to growth will enable you to navigate the complexities and opportunities artificial intelligence presents. Your exploration of AI does not end here. The insights and skills you have acquired lay the groundwork for continued growth and innovation. As you prepare to move forward, consider the broader implications of AI on society and the importance of ethical considerations in its application. Your understanding of AI's potential and limitations will guide your future endeavors, empowering you to contribute meaningfully to the evolution of technology and its impact on our world.

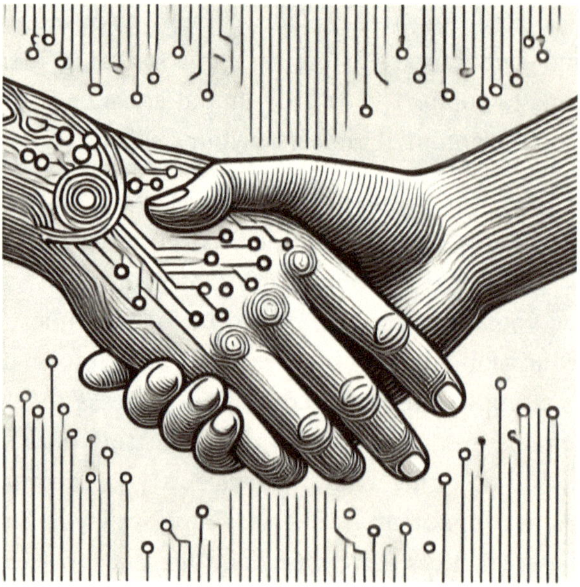

KEEPING THE GAME ALIVE

Now you have everything you need to confidently understand and embrace artificial intelligence—no tech skills required. You've unlocked the power of AI, learned how it shapes everyday life, and discovered practical ways to integrate this exciting technology into your personal and professional worlds.

It's time to share your newfound knowledge and help others discover the same confidence and clarity you've gained.

By leaving your honest opinion about this book on Amazon, you'll show other curious readers—everyday learners, busy professionals, entrepreneurs, and anyone else feeling a bit uncertain about technology—where they can find straightforward, easy-to-understand guidance on artificial intelligence.

Your review helps spread the passion for AI, empowering more people to thrive in an increasingly tech-driven world.

Thank you so much for your help. AI becomes even more powerful when we share our knowledge, and you're helping us keep this vital conversation alive.

Ready to make a difference?

Click here to leave your review on Amazon:

CONCLUSION

Throughout this book, we have embarked on a transformative journey into artificial intelligence. Together, we have demystified complex concepts, explored practical applications, and discovered AI's immense potential for shaping our personal and professional lives. As we conclude this exploration, I encourage you to reflect on the key insights you have gained and consider how you can harness AI's power to enrich your experiences.

At its core, AI is a tool that augments human capabilities, enabling us to solve problems more efficiently and make better-informed decisions. By understanding the fundamental principles of neural networks, machine learning, and natural language processing, you have laid the groundwork for meaningfully engaging with AI technologies. Whether it's leveraging AI-powered productivity tools, exploring creative applications, or staying informed about the latest advancements, you now possess the knowledge to navigate this exciting landscape with confidence.

One of the most essential takeaways from this book is the realization that AI is not a distant, abstract concept but a tangible presence in our daily lives. From personalized recommendations on streaming platforms to intelligent virtual assistants, AI is already enhancing our experiences in countless ways. By recognizing these applications and understanding the underlying technologies, you can make informed choices about integrating AI into your routines and workflows.

As you move forward on your AI journey, I encourage you to embrace a mindset of lifelong learning and curiosity. AI is constantly evolving, with breakthroughs and innovations emerging rapidly. By staying engaged with the latest developments, attending workshops and conferences, and participating in online communities, you can ensure that your knowledge remains current and relevant. This proactive approach to learning will benefit your personal growth and position you to seize new opportunities in an increasingly AI-driven world.

However, your AI journey does not end with acquiring knowledge alone. The true power of AI lies in its practical application. I urge you to take the insights you have gained from this book and put them into action. Experiment with AI tools and technologies that align with your interests and goals. Whether it's building a simple machine learning model, exploring AI-powered creative tools, or leveraging AI to streamline your work processes, hands-on experience is invaluable. By actively engaging with AI, you will deepen your understanding, develop new skills, and discover firsthand the transformative potential of this technology.

As you embark on this implementation path, remember that AI is not a replacement for human intelligence but rather a complement. The most successful applications of AI leverage the unique strengths of both humans and machines. You can achieve remarkable results by combining your creativity, intuition, and domain expertise with the computational power and pattern recognition capabilities of AI. Embrace the opportunity to collaborate with AI and explore how this symbiotic relationship can enhance your abilities and drive innovation in your field.

Finally, I encourage you to approach AI with a sense of responsibility and ethical consideration. As AI becomes increasingly integrated into our lives, we must ensure its development and deployment align with our values and promote the well-being of society as a whole. By staying informed about the ethical implications of AI, engaging in discussions about its societal impact, and advocating for responsible AI practices, you can contribute to shaping a future in which AI benefits all of humanity.

As you close this book, remember that your AI journey is beginning. The knowledge and insights you have gained are the foundation upon which you can build a lifelong exploration of this fascinating field. Embrace AI's opportunities, stay curious, and never stop learning. The future of AI is bright, and I am excited to see how you will contribute to shaping it.

Thank you for joining me on this journey, and I wish you all the best as you continue to explore the incredible world of artificial intelligence.

REFERENCES

Adam, F. (2024, July 3). AI Tools for Beginners: A Comprehensive Guide. Medium. Retrieved March 15, 2025, from https://medium.com/@fahmiadam/ai-tools-for-beginners-a-comprehensive-guide-0c71f4416d73

Babitz, K. (2024, December 20). AI in Retail: Transforming Efficiency, Personalization, and Customer Experience. Datacamp. Retrieved March 15, 2025, from https://www.datacamp.com/blog/ai-in-retail

CallMiner. (2024, April 28). 25 Examples of NLP & Machine Learning in Everyday Life. CallMiner. Retrieved March 15, 2025, from https://callminer.com/blog/25-examples-of-nlp-and-machine-learning-in-everyday-life

Carlson School of Management. (2024, May 17). Debunking 5 Artificial Intelligence Myths. Retrieved March 15, 2025, from https://carlsonschool.umn.edu/graduate/resources/debunking-5-artificial-intelligence-myths

Chui, M. (2023, August 1). The State of AI in 2023: Generative AI's Breakout Year. McKinsey. Retrieved March 15, 2025, from https://www.mckinsey.com/capabilities/quantumblack/our-insights/the-state-of-ai-in-2023-generative-ais-breakout-year

Coursera. (2024, March 19). 9 Real-Life Machine Learning Examples. Coursera. Retrieved March 15, 2025, from https://www.coursera.org/articles/machine-learning-examples

Coursera. (2025, March 14). Artificial Intelligence (AI) Terms: A to Z Glossary. Coursera. Retrieved March 15, 2025, from https://www.coursera.org/resources/ai-terms

Coursera Staff. (2025, January 28). Deep Learning vs. Machine Learning: A Beginner's Guide. Coursera. Retrieved March 15, 2025, from https://www.coursera.org/articles/ai-vs-deep-learning-vs-machine-learning-beginners-guide

Davenport, T., & Kalakota, R. (2019, June). The potential for artificial intelligence in healthcare. National Library of Medicine. Retrieved March 15, 2025, from https://pmc.ncbi.nlm.nih.gov/articles/PMC6616181/

Dopson, E. (2024, December 16). 11 Best AI Learning Platforms. Workramp. Retrieved March 15, 2025, from https://www.workramp.com/blog/ai-learning-platform/

Dutta Baruah, I. (2021b, July 21). Understanding the Basics of Neural Networks (for Beginners). Medium. Retrieved March 15, 2025, from https://medium.com/geekculture/understanding-the-basics-of-neural-networks-for-beginners-9c26630d08

Fuertes, R. A. (2025, February 21). Real-World Case Studies of Human-AI

Collaboration: Success Stories and Insights. Smyth OS. Retrieved March 15, 2025, from https://smythos.com/ai-agents/agent-architectures/human-ai-collaboration-case-studies/

Georgieva, K. (2024, January 14). AI Will Transform the Global Economy. Let's Make Sure It Benefits Humanity. IMF Blog. Retrieved March 15, 2025, from https://www.imf.org/en/Blogs/Articles/2024/01/14/ai-will-transform-the-global-economy-lets-make-sure-it-benefits-humanity

Glover, E. (2025, January 28). 33 Top Artificial Intelligence (AI) Apps to Know. Builtin. Retrieved March 15, 2025, from https://builtin.com/artificial-intelligence/ai-apps

hp. (2024, July 4). 5 Myth-Busting Facts about AI in the Workplace. CIO. Retrieved March 15, 2025, from https://www.cio.com/article/2512917/5-myth-busting-facts-about-ai-in-the-workplace.html

IBM Data and AI Team. (2023, October 16). Shedding light on AI bias with real world examples. IBM. Retrieved March 15, 2025, from https://www.ibm.com/think/topics/shedding-light-on-ai-bias-with-real-world-examples#:~:text=Examples%20of%20AI%20bias%20in%20real%20life,-As%20society%20becomes&text=Healthcare%E2%80%94Underrepresented%20data%20of%20women,black%20patients%20than%20white%20patients

Jones, A. (2022, August 16). GDPR Three Years Later: What Impact Has It Made? IS Partners. Retrieved March 15, 2025, from https://www.ispartnersllc.com/blog/gdpr-one-year-later-impact/

Kaggle: Your Machine Learning and Data Science Community. (2025). Kaggle. Retrieved March 15, 2025, from https://www.kaggle.com/

Kido, R. A. (2024, February 21). Real-World Case Studies of Human-AI Collaboration: Success Stories and Insights. Smyth OS. Retrieved March 15, 2025, from https://smythos.com/ai-agents/agent-architectures/human-ai-collaboration-case-studies/

Lang, K. (2024, April 9). 8 of the Best AI Productivity Tools to Help You Optimize How You Optimize How You Work. Buffer. Retrieved March 15, 2025, from https://buffer.com/library/ai-productivity-tools/

Marr, B. (2023, May 10). 15 Amazing Real-World Applications Of AI Everyone. Forbes. Retrieved March 15, 2025, from https://www.forbes.com/sites/bernardmarr/2023/05/10/15-amazing-real-world-applications-of-ai-everyone-should-know/

Putty, C. (2025, March 12). Examples of Artificial Intelligence (AI) in 7 Industries. thoughtful.ai. Retrieved March 15, 2025, from https://www.thoughtful.ai/blog/examples-of-artificial-intelligence-ai-in-7-industries

The Best AI Podcasts to Learn about AI. (2023). Messageheard. Retrieved March 15, 2025, from https://messageheard.com/mediahub/best-podcasts-ai

Tunell, A. (2024, July 3). We Tested 50+ AI Productivity Tools. Here Are The 16 Best Tools in 2025. Motion. Retrieved March 15, 2025, from https://www.usemotion.com/blog/ai-productivity-tools

www.ingramcontent.com/pod-product-compliance
Lightning Source LLC
Chambersburg PA
CBHW031352230926
51848CB00002B/494